D1461489

A Cambrian Way

Books by Richard Sale

A guide to the Cotswold Way (1980)
A visitor's guide to the Cotswolds (1982)
A walker's guide to Europe (1983)

Land over 250 metres (820 ft)

Route

0   10   50 miles
   10
                                               80 km

Richard Sale

A Cambrian Way

A personal guide to an unofficial route

Constable London

First published in Great Britain 1983
by Constable & Company Ltd
10 Orange Street London WC2H 7EG
Copyright © 1983 by Richard Sale
ISBN 0 09 462480 1
Set in Times Roman 9 pt by
Inforum Ltd, Portsmouth
Printed in Great Britain by
Pitman Press Ltd, Bath

To Nathan

Contents

Snowdonia National Park

Illustrations

Preface

The geographical structure of Wales is ideally suited to a
long-distance footpath, if we accept that such paths should
concentrate on high land. This suitability was recognised in the late
1960's by groups that had completed the 'construction' of the Offa's
Dyke path along the English-Welsh border. The possibility of such a
route, called the Cambrian Way from an early stage, was taken up
by the Countryside Commission, the official government arm for
designating long-distance footpaths, and by the Cambrian Way
Committee. The latter was a self-styled group representing leading
countryside groups, the Ramblers' Association and the Youth
Hostels Association, under the chairmanship of Tony Drake, a
leading member of both organisations. Tony Drake was largely
responsible for surveying a route which the Committee presented to
the Countryside Commission for consideration. This route was 'high
level', covering all the main mountain blocks in south and north
Wales. After it was challenged by several groups, the Commission
prepared a mainly lowland alternative for discussion. The Cambrian
Way Committee was unhappy with this, feeling, with justification,
that it failed to live up to the promise that Wales offered the walker.

The Commission was now in a difficult position. If it continued
with its proposed route it would antagonise those organisations in
favour of the path, while only marginally improving its position with
the major dissenters. If, instead, it accepted the Committee's route
it would antagonise those organisations opposed to the Way in
principle. The Commission's situation was not helped by the
adverse publicity that both the Cambrian Way and other long
footpaths were attracting in the walking press at that time. The
Commission attempted a compromise, appointing field officers to
survey all proposals in, first, south Wales, later in mid-Wales, but
never in north Wales.

It is not the intention of this book to continue the pro- and
anti-arguments for the path. Indeed this is entirely the wrong format

for such a discussion. Suffice it to say that the laudable attempt by the Commission to defuse the situation failed, and in early 1982 the project was abandoned.

Those influenced by the SGR system of French-speaking Europe, the Wanderweg of German Europe and the efforts of the European Ramblers' Association will be saddened by the decision. Those appalled by erosion and traffic on the Pennine Way will be heartened. The truth, if truth there be, must lie between these extremes. What the decision does mean is that anyone wanting to walk the length of Wales, from Cardiff to Conwy, can now make his own decision as to his route. This book offers the author's route, one which draws on his own work over many years, independent of both Commission and Committee, though drawing on their work also. It is a meandering route seeking interesting spots, scenic, mythical and historical, and exploring those aspects of the Welsh countryside.

The route follows rights of way and access – its status is considered in the Appendix on these points – but some requests and words of caution are necessary. In places it passes through isolated areas of considerable importance to the natural flora and fauna of Wales (and Britain). Almost throughout it passes across land that constitutes someone's personal livelihood. At all times it is imperative that the walker should consider the responsibility his presence places on him, not only in relation to the environment, but in relation to those who follow him and who will be judged by his actions. Access in Wales presents delicate problems, as do many of the scientific sites – be careful, disruption of the latter could prejudice the former.

The words of caution relate to the nature of the terrain. The route described is longer than the Pennine Way, and has twice that route's amount of climbing. If a single traverse is contemplated – and the book was not prepared with that in mind, what is described is an exploration not a route march – it will be arduous and the walker will need to be well equipped. The climatic section of the Appendix on Wales indicates that the decrease in temperature with altitude in upland Wales is higher than elsewhere. It also indicates that the upland areas are subject to rain and high winds which have the effect of reducing the apparent temperature by increasing convective heat losses from the body. In bad weather parts of the route are not easy to follow, and remember that there are no waymarks and the mapping here is not intended to be definitive.

That said, it is a worthwhile route, and the walker should greatly enjoy it. To derive the greatest pleasure he should be patient, perhaps visiting some parts more than once to savour seasonal effects. To those who complete it at one go, in twelve days, in continuous rain – congratulations. But you have missed the point.

Acknowledgements

From the point at which I first became interested in a long walk through Wales to the production of this book has been a long time. During that time many people, family and friends, have helped me, and it would be unfair to those whose contribution has temporarily escaped my memory to try and name them. To all of you – Thank you.

It would, however, be unfair not to mention certain individuals and organisations by name.

The county library services of Wales and the National Library of Wales have been unfailingly helpful.

John Tetlow was of considerable assistance on aspects of the southern part of the route.

On all aspects of the route I enjoyed the benefit of Tony Drake's vast experience. His assistance has also extended to the production of the technical part of the Appendix on rights of way.

I am grateful to Patrick Leeson for the skilfully drawn maps.

Finally I thank Mike Rogers for his companionship, encouragement and enthusiasm. In addition to these he has also contributed materially, two of the photographs being his work, and the Appendix on Welsh geology leaning heavily on his expertise.

A Note on Mapping
This is *not* a conventional guide-book. While every effort has been
made to keep the walker on the right track by furnishing sufficient
map references it is imperative that he possesses the relevant
Ordnance Survey maps. There is no waymarking on the route,
which means that walkers who stray off course will have difficulty in
regaining the route if they do not have their own maps. The relevant
maps are as follows:

1:25,000 First and Second Series
ST 17/27 Cardiff
ST 18 Caerphilly
ST 28/38 Newport (Gwent)
ST 29/39 Cwmbran
SO 20 Pontypool
SO 21 Abergavenny (West)
Brecon Beacons National Park (in 3 sheets)
1 Eastern Area – Abergavenny and the Black Mountains
2 Central Area – Brecon and the Beacons
3 Western Area – Llandeilo and the Black Mountain
SN 73 Llandovery
SN 74 Mynydd Mallen
SN 75 Llyn Berwyn
SN 76 Ystrad Meurig
SN 77 Devil's Bridge
SN 78 Ponterwyd
SN 79 Angler's Retreat
Snowdonia National Park (in 5 sheets)
1 Cader Idris/Dovey Forest
2 Harlech
3 Snowdon
4 Conwy Valley

Note
1 The double number sheets, e.g. ST 17/27, refer to second series
maps.
2 Some of the first series maps are out of date, e.g. SN 75 does not

show the Llyn Brianne reservoir.
3 The larger National Park maps have been indicated as they
represent a cheaper and more up-to-date method of acquiring
1:25,000 cover of these areas. The route does not traverse any part
of the 5th sheet (Bala) of the Snowdonia National Park series.

1:50,000 Series
171 Cardiff and Newport
161 Abergavenny and the Black Mountains
160 Brecon Beacons
147 Elan Valley and Builth Wells
135 Aberystwyth
124 Dolgellau
115 Caernarvon and Bangor

   A combination of the 1:50,000 series and 1:25,000 National Park
maps *should* be sufficient, as only the high barren plateau of
Elenydd would not then be covered at the larger scale. It goes
without saying that the wayfarer should be competent in the use of,
and should carry, a compass.
   Both map lists above read south-north. This is the preferred
direction of travel as the prevailing wind is south-west.
   The distances indicated in the circles on the maps are in
kilometres. The average walker, over mixed terrain, will achieve 5
kms per hour.

The Traveller in Wales

Wales has always attracted the traveller and the writings of those who have gone before can inspire the future wayfarer. Two such books have been companions to the writing of this one. First is the journey through, and description of, Wales by Giraldus Cambrensis – Gerald of Wales – Archdeacon of Brecon in the late twelfth century. Giraldus undertook his journey as companion to Baldwin, Archbishop of Canterbury, who was seeking support, in 1188, for the Third Crusade. Second is George Borrow's *Wild Wales*, a journey from a much later time. The first is, historically, of great interest, the second, though occasionally tedious, does contain some good insights, and includes excellent descriptive passages. That given below could hardly be improved on as a reason for walking in Wales:

> I turned and looked at the hills I had come across. There they stood, darkly blue, a rain cloud, like ink, hanging over their summits. Oh, the wild hills of Wales, the land of old renown and of wonder, the land of Arthur and Merlin!

For those who think it is a sacrilege that it is a piece of English prose that has been chosen to describe the attractions of upland Wales, here is the final section of a prose poem by John Ceiriog Hughes, a Welsh poet of the mid-nineteenth century. It expresses perfectly the call of the Welsh hills for all those who must return from their journeys to, and in, them:

> Son of the mountain am I,
> far from home making my song;
> But my heart is in the mountain,
> with the heather and small birds.

A Land, a People, a Language

A Land

Wales is a small country, in European terms, covering a little over 8,000 square miles. It is rectangular, 160 miles north-south, 50 miles east-west with the island of Anglesey (Ynys Mon) set off the northern coast and two western horns, the Lleyn Peninsula and old Pembrokeshire, enclosing Cardigan Bay. It is a mountainous country, lowland areas being restricted to valleys and the coastal plain, and it has produced a rugged nation.

Geologically the country is of great interest and the geology, together with its resultant geography and the effect of that geography on climate and social economics, is dealt with in Appendix I (page 247).

A People

Britain, taken as a whole, has been inhabited for at least 250,000 years, though it is almost certain that settlement has not been continuous, since that period has seen a number of ice ages that would have forced the inhabitants southward, as well as sculpting the land we see today. There is evidence in North Wales for the existence of Neanderthal Man or, more correctly, for articles with Mousterian associations, but the best known Welsh find is later – the Red Lady of Paviland. The Red Lady was the name given to the skeletal remains uncovered from a shallow grave in the entrance of a cave in cliffs at Paviland on the Gower peninsula. The remains were discovered by William Buckland, Dean of Westminster, in the early nineteenth century. The skeleton was stained red by ochre and was wrongly sexed, being in fact that of a young man. When he was alive the site would not have been at the sea's edge, the water having encroached on the plain that originally separated it from an inland cliff containing the cave. The reason for the red colouration is not known.

Remains from the age of the Red Lady are rare, which may show that the country received only minimal settlement. By the arrival of

Neolithic cultures, however, there was wide settlement, although it was grouped around the more hospitable lowlands – Anglesey, Ardudwy, the Glamorgan coastal plain. Many fine tombs have survived from this period. These can be normal long barrows, as at Tinkinswood near Cardiff or, more usually, the bare remnants of the rock slab tomb that underlay such mounds. These tombs, a capstone supported by a number of uprights, are normally called dolmens, but the Welsh word *cromlech* has been historically applied to all such monuments in Wales. The site at St. Lythans, near Cardiff, is a good one, but there are many others – Pentre Ifan in Pembrokeshire being considered one of the finest. Closer to the described route, the cromlechs of Gors-y-Gedol and Dyffryn Ardudwy, in the Ardudwy plain between the Rhinogs and Cardigan Bay, are also extremely interesting. In the same area are the Carneddau Hengwm, a pair of cromlechs and a pair of stone circles, one of the most concentrated sites in Wales. The tombs here are a little younger, representing a link between the Neolithic culture and that of the Bronze Age that replaced it. It is with the latter age that the large number of standing stones in Wales are usually associated, although that association is occasionally based on evidence which is, at best, flimsy. The Welsh for a standing stone is *maen hir*, long stone, and it is that name, shortened to menhir, that has become popular in describing such stones. Lately, with the increased coverage – not all of it useful – given to astro-archaeology, menhirs have taken on a considerable significance. It is now possible to view the stones as markers of extraterrestrial air terminals, batteries holding mystical power, or connections for large energy reservoirs. While such 'earth magic' ideas may be too fanciful, it is easy to understand the emotional tug of such stones. They stand, invariably, in dramatic sites and with the right weather conditions can represent a powerful image. The described route passes close to several, in the area around Mynydd Ddu, and also close to Cerrig Duon, a stone circle and alignment. No published work yet describes Cerrig Duon as a solar or lunar observatory, but the need to rationalise such sites is apparent when visiting it. It really is very intriguing why anyone should want to create such a pattern at such a site.

The replacement of the Bronze Age culture in Wales by the Iron

Age peoples appears to have been by intermixing rather than annihilation. This theory rests on two bases: first the finding, in Llyn Fawr, Glamorgan, of a hoard of metal objects, some of bronze, some of iron and yet of, apparently, contemporary manufacture and usage; and secondly, and more romantically, the possibility of a real folk memory behind the story of the lady of the lake that will be recounted when our journey reaches Llyn y fan fach. The Iron Age in Wales is deeply significant as it represents the coming of the peoples whose name is synonymous with the country – the Celts. The name does not appear to have been used by the people to describe themselves, but derives from the Roman *Keltoi*, which was interchangeable with *Galli* as the word used to describe the inhabitants of Gaul (France). The emergence of Celtic peoples would require a book in itself. For our purposes it is worthwhile noting only that proto-Celtic civilisations were of eastern and central European origin, the true iron-using Celtic cultures, first Hallstatt and later La Tène, being named from villages in Austria and Switzerland respectively.

To the civilised Romans and Greeks of Mediterranean Europe the Celts were barbarians, war-like savages. By comparison, of course, these descriptions were true, inter-tribal warfare being the apparent hallmark of the Celts (and later the downfall of the British), who also possessed no written language and worshipped strange gods. The Roman expansion into northern Europe was probably motivated as much by frequent attacks from the Celts on their border as by any expansionist dreams. The Romans were impressed by the qualities of the Celts in battle, but unimpressed by what they saw as the puerile boastings of their leaders, parading about in ornaments accompanied by men forever chanting their praises. They did not realise then the true significance of what they saw. The Celts, having no literature, had invested the history of their peoples in epic poems that were remembered and delivered by bards. This had two direct results. First a heroic leader stock was created which continually broadcast their own, and their ancestors', heroism. Thus a leader who was not rich and majestic, and not celebrated in the bardic poems, was suspect and might not protect you well enough. Secondly a love of language for its own sake

developed. To such an extent was this true that the Celts actually
had a god of eloquence – Ogmios. Eventually the Romans and
Greeks recognised this eloquence for what it was. The Celts
maintained, in essence, that the tongue was mightier than the sword
and they venerated age which increased its powers. Eventually they
emerged in the classical world as teachers of rhetoric.

The Celtic tribes had invaded Britain at an early time and were
well established when the Romans came. In many parts of Wales
the typical hill fort can be seen. The mystical site of Dinas Emrys is
on the described route, but the best site lies on Yr Eifl in the Lleyn
Peninsula, to the west of Snowdon. This is Tre'r Ceiri, the Town of
Giants, an immensely impressive array of fortifications and hut
circles.

The Roman invasion, that of AD 43 rather than the initial and
limited sortie of Julius Caesar, occurred for numerous reasons. It
secured the northern frontier for all time, cutting out any
possibilities of sea-borne surprise attacks; it conquered a land rich
in minerals; and, equally importantly, it allowed the creation of a
puppet state. To assist the last, the Romans played their trump card,
using the inter-tribal and, often, inter-hero disputes of the Celts to
their advantage. At the time southern England was effectively
controlled by Cunobelinus, king of the Catuvellauni from north of
the Thames, the Cymbeline of Shakespeare. According to
Shakespeare, and Geoffrey of Monmouth in his *History of the Kings
of Britain*, Cymbeline had two sons, Guiderius and Arviragus.
Modern scholars, however, see a dispute arising between other
sons, Amminius on the one hand, Caratacus and Togodumnus on
the other. In AD 40 Amminius was banished from Britain and
promptly sought the assistance of Rome. Cymbeline died and his
warlike sons expanded their kingdom at the expense of Verica king
of the Atrebates from south of the Thames. Verica too fled to
Rome. The Romans now had everything they needed, and they
invaded. Togodumnus was killed within the first weeks of the
invasion, but Caratacus fought fiercely and then escaped to Wales
where he rallied the Silures of South Wales and the Ordovices of
North Wales against the invader. He fought on until AD 51 when
he was betrayed and captured. It seems that his fighting ability and

his bearing after capture so impressed the Romans that he died peacefully as an honoured guest of Rome. The Romans clearly understood the Celts well enough not to relax when Caratacus was defeated, but to press on to Anglesey to destroy the seat of the Celtic priest class, the druids. Much has been written on the druids, and most of that is poor conjecture as there is no drawing of a druid extant, and no contemporary Celtic literature on the sect. This means that all descriptions, except by painstaking inference, are based on the written work of the Romans, who would hardly bend over backwards to portray the enemy's mainstay in a sympathetic light. Even the name of the sect is shrouded in mystery. It could derive from 'oak-tree' since it is known that certain druidic rituals were associated with the oak, particularly the (rare) mistletoe-bearing trees; or it could derive from 'sees far', denoting the likely role of the sect as seers and magicians and, perhaps, holders of sacred information on seed sowing times or eclipses. Whatever the druids were the Romans destroyed them in Anglesey. Tacitus portrays the sad scene of the soldiers of Rome confronted by a priesthood whose only weapon was ritual cursing: the anger of Celtic deities proved no match for the short sword.

After the Roman conquest Britain was quiet for several centuries, the local Celtic tribes becoming Romanised and the basis of the present system of roads and towns being created. When the Romans finally withdrew, however, the British proved that they had learnt nothing in the occupation years and there was an immediate return to tribalism with new kings emerging to do battle with each other. Such a system of small states with little cohesion and occasional open hostility was easy to deal with, and the Anglo-Saxon invaders pushed the British farther and farther west during the period between AD 400, when the Romans departed, and AD 500, when the second name synonymous with Wales occurs, for around that time King Arthur reigned. The historical sources that point to the existence of Arthur are small in number and open to interpretation. The volumes of words that have been written about him are countless. It would be pointless in this introduction to attempt to unravel the truth, or even to explore the myth – although this is touched on in the main text where appropriate. For our purposes here it is sufficient to note that the first influx of Saxons into Britain had been requested by a British king, Vortigern, to help him in a tribal dispute. Unfortunately the Saxons had stayed and gradually pushed westward. Under Arthur, if he existed at all then, a war lord rather than a king, the Saxons had been halted conclusively at the battle of Badon (near the Ridgeway?) around AD 500. If there is any truth in the Arthurian stories, Arthur himself then fell victim to a tribal dispute and the Saxons were free to march again. In 577 they won the battle of Dyrham, near Bristol, cutting the country in half and banishing the British to Cornwall and Wales. England and Wales had been created, and not just as geographical entities. The Saxons saw the British to the west of the Severn as the Wallas, foreigners. The root of the name is another Celtic tribe, the Velcae, known to the Saxons though strangers to them. The root gives us Walloons in Belgium; Valais in Switzerland; the German name for Italians – Velsch; Vlachs in Romania; and Welsh in Wales. The British, now isolated from their own kind, increasingly stopped referring to themselves as Brythons (Britons), being instead 'fellow countrymen', Cymry.

However it should not be assumed that the population of Wales at this time was simply the remnants of British tribes from England, for that is not the case. The Saxon thrust had ended at the Severn and while Wales almost certainly collected refugees it contained also the still-intact kingdoms that had existed since the departure of the Romans. The Saxon invasion had not harmed them, merely isolated them. Wales was now left in peace while the Saxons moved northward to secure a strong northern border. This was a long process and the Saxons lost interest in westward expansion. Eventually an effective demarcation line was set up between Saxon England and Wales by the construction of a boundary dyke by the Mercian king Offa. The true reason for the construction of the dyke, an earthwork which stretched 160 miles from the northern coast near Prestatyn to Chepstow, is not known. Certainly it would have acted as a barrier to raiding parties, but it might also have been a frontier, that is a trading barrier and agreed boundary. Beyond the dyke the Celtic Welsh continued their favourite sport of inter-tribal strife tempered during the pre-Norman period by the activities of the Christian saints.

The saints were very active, roaming the country preaching and setting up small religious centres, the llanau. Each llan was an earthwork, or wooden church, and their existence has passed into the language, the names being passed on to the towns that grew up around the sites. Through the place names we are familiar, without always realising it, with the activities of St. David, St. Illtud and many others. While the saints created the village framework, the people moving out of their hill-top forts, the kingdoms of Wales were developing. The new counties of Wales have names that derive from these kingdoms: Gwynedd, Powys, Dyfed and Gwent. Greatest of all was Gwynedd, a mountain kingdom that possessed two vital factors for a defensible unit, the mountains of Snowdon as a barrier and the fertile lowlands of Anglesey as a granary. While other kingdoms were important at times and their kings held great power occasionally, it is Gwynedd that is consistently at the forefront of Welsh power, and the Gwynedd kings who dominate Welsh history. In the early years of Wales as a separate entity, say from 550 onwards, the lineage of Cunedda held Gwynedd. This line included Maelgwn, the dragon, a physically immense man of apparently limitless violence, and finished with Rhodri Mawr, . sometimes called the first king of all Wales. This he was not though by his death he did control Gwynedd, Powys and most of Ceredegion (the old county of Cardigan). He did not, however, rule Gwent, Morgannwg, Dyfed or Brycheiniog (Breconshire). On his death his own kingdom was, as customary, divided between his sons and Wales lost another chance of unification in a welter of warfare. Another, later, king who is also occasionally credited with uniting Wales is Hywel Dda, Hywel the Good, who united Ceredegion and Dyfed as Deheubarth, and then took Gwynedd and Powys. He also failed to secure Gwent, Morgannwg and Brycheiniog. Hywel is best remembered for his codification of Welsh law, a code that far outlived him. In addition to this justly renowned work, Hywel also laid down the duties of the royal household servants. The strangeness of the times relative to our own is shown in the fact that the latter code included rules for the Royal Footholder, who sat under the table and scratched Hywel's foot when required. In

general, to see Hywel as 'the good' you have to ignore the great
violence of his actions.

Ultimately Wales was unified, by Grufydd, son of Llywelyn ap
Seisyllt. Grufydd ap Llywelyn succeeded by inheritance, marriage
and violence – the usual mixture – and by 1041 he controlled the
whole country. Almost immediately Grufydd over-reached himself
and sought allegiances with Saxon lords near the dyke, probably in
an effort to expand eastward. Earl Harold Godwinson convinced
Edward the Confessor that the Welsh king represented a threat and
received permission to move against him. Earl Harold invaded
Wales subduing the south and then moving north in pursuit of
Grufydd with hand-picked troops. These were not intimidated by
the terrain of Gwynedd and Grufydd was killed. Wales fragmented
again and by the time the Normans arrived at the dyke there was
once more a system of small, squabbling kingdoms on its western
side. The Normans never pressed ahead with a conquest of Wales, it
apparently not being part of William's plan for his new realm.
Instead he installed along the dyke, on the march, or boundary, of
England and Wales, a line of barons, the marcher lords. These lords
ruled virtually independent states, and their westward boundaries
were of their own choosing. Consequently they encroached on
Welsh land perpetually, gradually pushing the "free" Welsh back
towards Gwynedd. There, typically, the Welsh made a last stand for
independence. Owain Gwynedd pushed the Normans back across
Powys, but was defeated and forced back. Equally typically,
Owain's death caused a power struggle and a weakening of
Gwynedd, but his grandson Llywelyn ap Iorwerth (Llywelyn the
Great) succeeded to the kingdom in 1203 and strengthened it. He
conquered Powys and by siding with the English barons gained
rights for Wales in Magna Carta. He had successes in South Wales
and when he died in 1240 the country, while not unified, had a truly
independent air. It had been a considerable achievement. The lack
of unity caused fragmentation but Llywelyn's grandson Llywelyn ap
Grufydd (Llywelyn the Last) campaigned again for Welsh unity. He
demanded, and received, the title Prince of Wales from Henry III
under the treaty of Montgomery of 1267 and the future looked as
good as at any time since the Normans had arrived. Sadly Edward I

was of sterner stuff than his predecessors and invaded Wales to force a submission and homage from Llywelyn. This he received at the Treaty of Aberconwy in 1277 which reduced Llywelyn's position to that of a baron. In 1282 Llywelyn rose again, but briefly, being killed in a minor skirmish near Builth Wells. A stone marks the spot where the last Welsh Prince of Wales fell. Llywelyn's brother Dafydd continued the struggle but was captured in 1283 and executed for treason.

Edward decided that never again should the royal house of Wales, or the Welsh, represent a threat to England. The castles of the ring of stone are a tangible reminder of this decision. But additionally Edward systematically removed the lineage of the Welsh royal houses by forcing women into nunneries and preventing men from producing heirs by long-term imprisonment or death. It was, in the main, a humane elimination, in comparison with the violence of the age. Recognising the need in the Welsh for a prince, he gave them, at Caernarfon, a prince 'who could speak no word of English'. The modern Welsh view of this affair, which is not sympathetic, disregards the fact that at the time the Welsh appreciated the gesture and were favourably impressed. To prove the point there was peace in Wales for a hundred years, a peace that was shattered only when a personal feud boiled over into national rebellion. This rebellion, of Owain Glyndwr, is dealt with more fully in the main text as several of the most important sites in his campaign for an independent Wales are on the route. Ultimately Glyndwr failed leaving the country ravaged. True peace with England seemed as far away as ever but it came in dramatic style when the Welsh family of Tudor supplied England and Wales with a king in 1485, Harri Tewdwr, Henry VII. Thereafter Welsh history and English history coincide politically.

Socially that was not quite so, however, with rural Wales being a poor country until very recent times. The industrialisation of North Wales, for slate, and South Wales, for coal and steel, followed the Victorian English fashion of exploitation giving the Welsh an equality with their English counterparts that they might not have recognised as such. Wales has retained elements of its culture, however, as a trip to an Eisteddfod will show, and recognition of this has led, in the recent past, to an upsurge of nationalism with equality for the language as its central theme.

A Language

The language of the 'foreigners' of 'Wales' has its roots, as one would expect, in the Celtic languages of continental Europe. As such it shares a common ancestry with the Teutonic based English language, though there is little obvious similarity now, many centuries after the split. The Celtic language that crossed from the continent was itself subject to a split, the Goidelic language group occurring in Ireland, the isle of Man and Scotland, the Brythonic language dominating in the rest of Britain and, therefore, yielding the Welsh and Cornish dialects. The Breton language of French Brittany is also a Brythonic language. To differentiate between the Goidelic, i.e. Gaelic, and Brythonic languages the former is called Q Celtic, the latter P Celtic, the reason being the pronounciation of 'qu'. Q Celtic pronounces this as 'qu' or, rather, 'c', while P Celtic pronounces it 'p'. Thus, in mountain terms, Welsh has 'pen' while Gaelic has 'ceann'.

To the English eye the Welsh language is an unreadable mass of vowel-less words, consonants back-to-back. This is, of course, not so, but based on the misconception that the alphabets of the two languages are the same. In fact Welsh has extra consonants, dd, ll and ff being letters – not as strange as it seems, for remember that English has w, i.e. uu – and can utilise w and y as vowels. While dd and ll have their own sounds – the former as 'th'; the latter as 'thl' – ff is pronounced f, the Welsh f being pronounced v. Thus Tryfan is pronounced Tryvaen. Also cwm (mountain hollow) is acceptable, and pronounced coom. A second, and radical, departure from English is initial mutation, the alteration of the initial consonants of words when the final sound of the preceding word is of particular form. The reason for this appears to be straightforwardly aesthetic. However the (apparently random) interchangeability of, say, fawr and mawr (large) or fach and bach (small), not to mention other worse forms, e.g. cam – gam – ngham – cham, makes the casual observer wince.

Despite this explanation, however, the English visitor on his first

trip to Wales will sympathise with Nathaniel Hawthorne, the
nineteenth-century American writer. He visited Bangor and wrote:
'At Bangor we . . . hired a carriage and two horses for some Welsh
place, the name of which I forget; neither can I remember a single
name of any of the places through which we posted on that day, nor
could I spell them if I heard them pronounced, nor pronounce them
if I saw them spelt.'

The visitor has less trouble with Welsh names, Christian or
surnames. Indeed the lack of trouble seems to be the fact that there
appear to be only half-a-dozen surnames in the whole of Wales. The
story immediately comes to mind of the Welsh male voice choir
refused entry to an East European country because the frontier
guard would not believe that there was not a decadent western plot
behind a large group of men, ninety per cent of whom were called
Davies! The story is told that a judge touring Wales became so
appalled by the stream of plaintiffs and defendants with names such
as Rhys ap Llewellyn, Taliesin ap Iorewerth and worse, that he
decreed that the naming system should be rationalised –

> Take ten, he said, and call them Rice
> Take another ten and call them Price
> Now Roberts name some hundred score
> And Williams name a legion more
> And call, he moaned in languid tones,
> Call the other thousands – Jones

It is a charming tale, and the Welsh names have a charm, one
accentuated by their delight in double naming – Robert Roberts,
Evan Evans, and Thomas Thomas, the redoubtable Twm
Dwywaith, Tom Twice. Equally delightful is the use of the
descriptive name – Williams the Milk, Jones the Post and the more
comical ones, the undertaker – Dai the Death.

To attempt a comprehensive glossary of useful Welsh names
would be doomed to failure. Throughout, the common form of
place-name has been used, e.g. Cardiff rather than Caerdydd.
Listed below are those that will allow the first visitor to understand
the area he is traversing a little better.

Aber – confluence, but usually a river mouth

Afon – river

Allt – hill, especially if wooded

Bach, Fach, Bychan – small

Ban – peak or horn

Bedd – grave

Blaen – head of valley

Bont – bridge

Bwlch – pass

Cadair – chair

Capel – chapel

Carreg – stone

Cefn – ridge

Coch – red

Coed – wood

Craig – crag

Cwm – mountain hollow, a valley with a backslope, as in the famous usage in Western Cwm below Everest

Dinas – town or hill-fort ·

Diolch – thank you

Du, Ddu – black

Dwr – water

Dyffryn – valley

Eglwys – church

Esgair – long ridge

Ffordd – road, pathway

Ffynnon – well, spring

Glas, Las – blue-green

Gors – bog

Gwyn – white

Gwynt – wind

Hafod – summer dwelling, hill-side house for summer use

Hen – old

Hendre – winter dwelling, valley house for winter use

Hir – long

Isaf – lowest

Llech – flat stone

Llwybr Cyhoeddus – public footpath

Llwyd – grey

Llyn – lake

Maen – stone (Maen Hir – long stone or standing stone, i.e. Menhir)

Moel, Foel – bare hill

Mynydd, Fynydd – mountain

Nant – stream, brook

Ogof – cave

Pant – small hollow

Pen – peak

Pistyll – waterfall, usually a water spout

Plas – mansion

Porth – gate

Pwll – pool

Rhaiadr – waterfall

Sarn – causeway

Tref – town

Ty – house

Uchaf – highest

Waun – moor

Ynys – island

And remember, Dynion is for men, Merched is for ladies.

The Valleys

Cardiff

It is fitting that a walk exploring Wales, even if only by way of its
highland backbone, should start at the capital. As a capital,
however, Cardiff (Caerdydd) has a very recent history, having
acquired that position by royal decree as lately as 1955. As a town
Cardiff has had a long if somewhat spasmodic history. The area
around the town, that is the coastal plain of the rivers that drain the
Glamorgan upland plain – the Rhymney, the Taff and the Ely – has
very few sites dating from pre-Roman times. Between the villages of
St. Nicholas and St. Lythans that lie about 4 miles to the south-west
of Llandaff are the remains of two Neolithic long-barrows. One of
these, nearer to St. Lythans, consists of a capstone supported by
three uprights. The mound that once covered this burial chamber
has long since shrunk to just a trace. Such structures, of which there

The neolithic burial chamber near St. Lythans village, four miles south-west of Cardiff.

are several in Wales, are known as Cromlechs. St. Lythans is
supposed to have supernatural qualities, the capstone rising up and
turning three times once each year. The other barrow, taking its
name from the nearby hamlet of Tinkinswood, is more complete,
and with its dry-stone walling and hornwork near the entrance is a
clear indication of continuity with the builders of the long barrows
in the Cotswolds to the east of the Severn. The earliest settlers were
gradually replaced, culturally, by the Iron Age (early Celtic)
invaders from Continental Europe. The western Celts maintained a
strong hold on their heritage, and by the time of the Roman
invasion of Britain the difference between the Silures of South
Wales and the semi-Romanised Belgic tribes of southern England
was quite clear. The farther the Romans advanced from the
southern coast the more difficult the task became. Having secured
the Cotswolds the Romans advanced into south Wales in order to
subdue the Silures. Since the Romans had invaded Britain more
with an eye to its economic potential than to secure its northern
frontier, this advance into Wales was probably driven as much by its
mineral wealth as the need to secure the Severn boundary, though
the Silures' frequent incursions, and the potential power base of the
druids in Anglesey, would have been considerations. As usual the
first bases were military, including that at Cardiff, at a crossing of
the Taff.

   With the subjugation of the Silures, Cardiff became less
important, particularly as the pleasant town of Venta Silurum (the
market town of the Silures), as Caerwent was then known, was so
close. Excavations in Cardiff – the original Roman fort stood on the
same site that the castle now occupies – show a spasmodic
occupation from about AD 70 through to the mid-fourth century.
Then, briefly, the town became important once more, a more
substantial fort being built to help defend the area against the
sea-borne invaders from the west. Eventually as thrusts against
Rome itself increased the Romans evacuated Britain and left the
Romanised British to defend themselves against the Saxons. It is
likely that Cardiff was abandoned at that time, though the British
name Caer Tyf – the fort by the Taff – indicates that there may have
been intermittent use of the site. The British contained the Saxon

advance to the west side of the Severn for a long period aided, at some stage, by the exploits of the real Arthur. Legend has it that Cardiff was the site of embarkation of Sir Lancelot for France, and of Arthur himself in pursuit. More mundanely the area was held by descendants of Maximus, the last Roman ruler, and successfully defended after the battle of Dyrham, near Bath, which effectively created England under Saxon rule as a separate entity from Wales under British rule. A tenth-century descendant of Maximus, Morgan Mwynfawr, gave his name to the land around Cardiff – Morgannwg, the land of Morgan – which has remained to this day, Anglicised as Glamorgan.

The area remained in British hands until the coming of the Normans. Cardiff was visited by William the Conqueror in 1081 as he travelled to St. David's on a pilgrimage. Indeed a local chronicler maintains that William founded the town at that time. It was not until the very late eleventh century however that a realistic attempt was made to subjugate the area when Robert Fitzhamon, the Norman lord of Gloucester, crossed the Severn. Fitzhamon constructed a 'motte and bailey' castle on the site of the Roman fort. As a marcher lord he was able to annexe as much land as he believed he could hold and this he duly did, installing at intervals his own knights on feudal estates. This had the advantage of protecting the main town, and Fitzhamon's own home, of Cardiff behind a Norman frontier and sharing out the burden of defence. The defence was not always adequate and the town was attacked several times, most crucially by followers of Owain Glyndwr in 1404.

Glyndwr is an enigmatic character whose name is met at many points throughout Wales. Farther north our route takes us through Machynlleth where he held a parliament proclaiming his intention to promote learning by the establishment of a Welsh University, among other worthy ideas. Here at Cardiff the other side of the man was revealed when his army burst in through the city's west gate and laid waste to the town, firing it before departing. The scars of the attack remained for almost a century such was its ferocity.

Following the Acts of Union of 1536 and 1542 some of the privileges held by the marcher lords were removed. The effect of this was to limit the local warfare in the area. The securing of a

The Norman keep, Cardiff Castle

stable Glamorgan, and indeed a stable South Wales, was of
paramount importance to the English throne. The lesson of the
landing of a French army at Milford Haven had been learned hard,
but well. The peace that followed the Acts lasted until the whole of
South Wales was caught up in Civil War. The lord of the manor at
Cardiff, Philip, Earl of Pembroke was staunchly Parliamentarian, at
odds with the majority in the area. By 1645 however, particularly
after the battle of Naseby, the locals were disenchanted. It was not
that they had become followers of Parliament, more that they saw
the inevitability of defeat. King Charles arrived at Cardiff himself in
late July 1645 clearly expecting to be able to raise yet another army
to continue to fight for a lost cause. He stayed a week during which
time it was made abundantly clear to him that the County of
Glamorgan did not share his view of the future. On 4 August the

King left for Brecon for another attempt to raise an army. He was obviously deeply depressed, but he was also becoming divorced from reality. His failure to sue for peace at this time is clear indication of this, and so too was his comment that 'the hearts of the people of Wales are as hard and rocky as their country'. Such a comment showed an appalling lack of sensitivity. The Welsh had been suppressed for centuries and, for the greater part of that time, had had good reason to dislike the English; the Act of Union had merely legitimised what was in reality a conquest obtained on occasions in bloody fashion. Despite all this they had joined the King in droves and followed his cause, for the most part badly equipped, to their deaths. In 1648 they did manage to raise an army, in the Second Civil War, to assist the dissatisfied Parliamentarian army of West Wales to revolt against the army of Cardiff. The division of the Parliamentarian forces was on ideological grounds, but the Royalists were quick to seize the opportunity. Sadly the rising was short-lived when their eastward march was halted at St. Fagan's just west of Cardiff. There in an appallingly bloody battle by the river Ely the Royalists and their new allies were annihilated. Such was the slaughter that it was said that the river Ely actually (rather than fancifully) ran red.

Following the restoration of the monarchy the power of Parliament remained decisive and the time was right for Cardiff to emerge as a commercial town, rather than just a fortification on the Taff river. At this time, however, the wealth of the great mining valleys to the north of the town had not been truly realised. There was some movement of coal, but Cardiff was remote from the production sites, and mining itself was not well developed. Production was mainly from the working of surface seams, and even that was carried out on a largely *ad hoc* basis. The factors that were radically to increase the importance of Cardiff were the development of better mining techniques and the discovery of coking coal which allowed coal to replace charcoal in the smelting of iron. Both of these developments led to the construction of ironworks in the valleys to the north of the town. What the ironworks needed was a port, and the obvious choice was Cardiff. This led to the construction, in the mid-eighteenth century, of the

Cardiff Centre

Glamorgan canal from the Cynon valley down to Cardiff itself, and to the construction of dock facilities at the town. The impetus for the expansion of the port was the European wars of the late eighteenth and early nineteenth centuries when the London (Woolwich) arsenal required iron in great quantities, as much as 100,000 tons being delivered annually. This increase in dockland activity brought also an increase in industrial activity.

Coincidentally there arrived in Cardiff a family which was to have a significant and lasting influence on the town – the Butes. On the industrial side the Butes constructed, at an early stage, the first docks so that larger boats could use the port, in the hope that there would be an increase in coal export. This was a relatively successful venture but trade was still slow, as it depended on coal barges on the canal. As the canal was both narrow and shallow, the competition between coal and iron barges was intense. Resolution of the problem came in 1840 with the opening of the first part of the Taff Valley Railway. It is ironic that this development, which so materially affected the wealth of Cardiff, was opposed by the canal company who had to be handsomely compensated for the loss of revenue, despite having been unable to cope with the volume of traffic in the immediate pre-railway years.

The improvement in the delivery of coal to the town (3 million tons annually by 1870) required further expansion of the docks and the Butes constructed the massive East Dock, complete with the most modern coal-loading equipment. Recognition of the docks as one of the most modern in the area attracted considerable industry to the area and that, together with the finance, insurance and other commercial ventures that grow up around such heavily industrialised areas, caused a rapid expansion in population, building and wealth. Again the Butes were instrumental, land to the west of their dockland complex being used for the construction of Butetown. This area was later to become famous as Tiger Bay, birthplace of many Welsh legends, some mythical, some based on real life. Now Tiger Bay has gone, as has the majority of the coal export trade that made Cardiff rich.

From a visitor's point of view it is the magnificent civic centre of Cathays Park that marks Cardiff as a capital city, the site being

City Hall dome and clock tower, Cathays Park, Cardiff

capable of withstanding comparison with those of any other capital – large and airy, with an array of elegant buildings. It is surprising to hear therefore that the site was purchased by the town from the Bute family as long ago as the turn of the century, fully half a century before the declaration of capital status. This remarkably far-sighted venture by the town deserved to succeed; and so it has – the effect of the Portland stone buildings and the wide avenues, with parkland, statues, fountains and memorials set on a site of 100 acres being a brilliant centrepiece to the city. The City Hall itself was the first building to be opened, in 1905. The clock tower, at almost 200 feet, and the fierce Welsh dragon on the dome dominate the outside of the building, while inside the Marble Hall contains a series of statues commemorating Welsh heroes. One year after completion of the City Hall the Law Courts were completed, although it was a further 20 years before the southern edge of the complex was completed by the opening of the National Museum of Wales, an imposing structure with a large dome. Inside there is the National Art Collection containing a number of very rare items. The building also contains exhibits on the geography, geology, natural history and archaeology of Wales. The National Museum has several outlying sites, most notably that at St. Fagans, near Llandaff, which will be mentioned later. Within the city, at Bute Street in the dock area, is the Industrial and Maritime Museum including a collection of engines and some exhibits from the early maritime history of the area.

Between the Museum and the City Hall is Museum Avenue, to the east of which lies the University College of South Wales and Monmouthshire, the largest of the colleges that constitute the University of Wales. This was opened in 1909, although it has been greatly extended since. Between the City Hall and the Law Courts is King Edward VII Avenue, to the west of which is the County Hall, opened in 1912, with a very imposing facade complete with Corinthian pillars. The rear of the building, on North Road beside Bute Park, is equally imposing. Near the County Hall are the Registry of the University of Wales and the South Wales Police Headquarters, opened in 1968. Despite the inscription the building was not, in fact, opened by James Callaghan, the local M.P. who was at the time Home Secretary and later, of course, Prime Minister. Mr. Callaghan was prevented from attending by the crisis over the Russian invasion of Czechoslovakia and the opening was performed by Lord Stanham. Farther along the Avenue is the Temple of Peace and Health. Lord Davies of Llandinam presented the building to the people of Wales in 1938, an auspicious year in view of the purpose of the building, which was to be the centre of the Welsh campaign against war and disease. It was the first building in Britain to be so dedicated, and houses Welsh councils to the U.N. and other international organisations. Beyond the Temple is the University of Wales Institute of Science and Technology, a new arm of the University created by the giving of a charter to the local Technical College. Opposite the Temple is the Welsh Office. Between the two Avenues is an area of quiet parkland containing the National War Memorial

The west wing, Cardiff Castle

Within sight of the Civic Centre is the castle. As we have seen the first fort was Roman. Initially this would have been a simple, and quickly erected, defensive structure, though later a more impressive fort covering 8 acres was erected. This would have been a square of earth ramparts topped by a wooden fence containing the army barracks. At a later stage the walls were constructed of stone, as much as 10 feet thick in places, and these form the basis of the rectangular structure we see today. The Normans repaired this basic Roman form and added the mound, or motte, and the keep that surmounts it. The mound was given a moat for further protection, and very soon after construction was used as a prison for Robert, Duke of Normandy, captured by Henry I at Tinchebrai in 1106. Robert was held here for the last 28 years of his life, the misery of his existence being increased substantially by the decision that the

keep, moat and walls were insufficiently strong and that his eyes
should be put out 'for greater security'. A thirteenth-century
addition was the Black Tower near the main gate which was also
used as a prison, entry to a windowless, airless cell being by a trap
door in the tower floor. Between the keep and the tower ran a
defensive wall dividing the castle into inner and outer wards. Much
of this work is still visible, the keep being reached by crossing the
moat and climbing up the steep mound. At the same time as the
castle defences were increased the town was walled completely,
except for its western side which was adequately protected by the
river Taff. Some idea of the size of the medieval town can be gained
by considering the position of the gates. The eastern gate was at the
eastern edge of the castle wall, the west was near the junction of
Duke Street and Queen Street, and the south gate was near the
church of St. Mary, which has also since disappeared but is
commemorated in St. Mary's Street.

The most striking additions to the castle were made by the third
Marquess of Bute, who employed the architect William Burges to
construct what is now the south-western corner of the castle. Burges
added the Clock Tower, an ornate 150-feet square-sided tower, and
the Bute Tower, a lower square tower topped by a roof garden, to
the wall which already contained the Octagonal Tower from the
mid-fifteenth century and the Hubert Tower from the sixteenth
century. He also added an internal western wing of domestic rooms.
These can be visited, as can the Bute Tower roof gardens in the
summer months, and are an amazing spectacle. Taken together the
wing has been described as one of the triumphs of
nineteenth-century Romantic architecture, though it was the
richness of the internal work that attracted most attention. It is a
magical array of panelling and statuary, plasterwork and glass. The
whole effect, which starts with peacocks on the lawn outside who
seem sombre by comparison, is beyond description and should not
be missed. The same architect, William Burges, also restored
Castell Coch, which will be passed on the way north of Cardiff, and
which is equally, if not more, remarkable.

A little way south-east of the castle, which was given to the City
by the Bute family in 1948, is St. John's church, overtopped and

hemmed in by modern buildings, but retaining the humble dignity of a site which is the oldest centre of worship now remaining in the town. It was originally built as a chapel of ease for the now vanished church of St. Mary's. There is some early (thirteenth-century) work on the south chancel arcade but extensive work was required following the sacking of the town by Glyndwr. What we now see is the fifteenth-century re-building in the Perpendicular style, though there have been enlargements at later stages, particularly when St. Mary's was lost in the Taff flooding of 1607 and St. John's became the parish church. In the Hubert chapel there is a fine Jacobean monument to two of the Hubert family whose name is commemorated in the castle tower. Near to the door of the screen that surrounds the chapel are carved two small heads, a man and a woman each with its tongue out. Legend has it that these are the Roman soldier in charge of the Crucifixion, and the wife of the Jerusalem blacksmith who, when her husband refused to make nails for the Crucifixion, made them herself.

The church tower was described, in the late sixteenth century, as 'a very faire steeple . . . The workmanship of it, being carried to a great heighth, and above beautifyed with Pinnacles, of all skillfull beholders is very well liked of'. For nearly 80 years around the turn of the nineteenth century the area beneath was used to house the town fire engine.

Cardiff Castle can be seen as a natural starting point for our route, particularly for those intending to journey all the way to the Castle of Conwy. A fine piece of walking then commences the journey, through Bute Park sandwiched between the river Taff and the Castle. Close to here, to the south of Castle Street, and also standing alongside the river, is that monument to Welshness, the Arms Park containing the ground of Cardiff Rugby Club as well as the National Stadium. The site is named from an old inn – the *Arms Park* – that stood here, but is now virtually a shrine to the national game. For such a small nation Wales has a truly remarkable record in its domination of the game, due in no small part to the fervour with which it is followed in the southern valleys. This fervour is almost religious in the crowd during matches, with massed voices singing hymns to support the home team's display.

Bute Park is one of the many parks in Cardiff, the open green areas being such a feature of the city. Farther north-east in Roath, is a 100-acre park set around a 32-acre lake. The lake has a lighthouse which commemorates the departure from Cardiff in 1910 of Scott's ill-fated expedition to Antartica. Over the river from Bute are the Pontcanna fields and Sophia Gardens. At the southern end of Bute Park are the remains of the priory of Blackfriars, as the Dominican monks were known. Both they and the Greyfriars, the Franciscans, had houses in the medieval town, there now being no remains of the Greyfriar house to the east of the castle. Both houses were dissolved on a day in September 1538.

Near the remains of the priory is a Gorsedd, as this modern circle of stones is known. The stones are linked with the Eisteddfodau, and appear also to be linked with antiquity – the ancient stone circles of pre-Celtic times. Sadly such is not the case. It all started in London in 1792 when the 'Gentleman's Magazine' recorded that on 23 September, 'This being the day on which the autumnal equinox occurred, some Welsh Bards, resident in London, assembled in congress . . . according to ancient usage . . . a circle of stones formed, in the middle of which was the Maen Gorsedd, or altar . . .'. This conclave was organised by Edward Williams, a Glamorgan stone-mason living in London. Williams had an interest in Welsh culture, history and poetry. He had adopted the bardic title Iolo Morgannwg, and by skilful forgery produced documents which 'proved' that the Glamorgan bards had preserved ceremonies of the original druids. Such forgeries, and the strange ritual of the Gorsedd, would have had little impact on Welsh tradition had Williams not managed to persuade the organisers of the Eisteddfod – then going through a period of decline – that the fake ceremony was real and a necessary addition to their assembly. Consequently the Gorsedd is now set up at a site a year and a day before the Eisteddfod for the ritual pronunciation. The ceremony, because of Williams' forgeries, is inexorably tied up with the druids, and is therefore carried out by 'druidic' figures in full regalia. Since no writings or pictures of the druids are extant the regalia is pure invention consisting of oak leaves, various sceptres and some jewellery based on that of the Bronze Age (i.e. pre-druid). Nor are the Gorsedd druids the only group claiming descendancy from the Celtic priesthood, there having been a number set up, mainly during the Victorian revival of interest in pre-history. None has any better, or worse, claim than the Welsh group and in general true historical perspective has been clouded by their activities, particularly their bogus rites at Stonehenge, which pre-dates the original druids by two thousand years. The Welsh Eisteddfod (the plural is Eisteddfodau), is a genuinely ancient and worthwhile gathering involving musical and literary competition and, more recently, cultural exchange. It is sad that it has become embroiled in such a collection of forged rites.

For the remainder of the walk through Bute Park the walker is freed from such contentious sites as he follows the river Taff through to the main A48 road. The river is a fine sight here, and in its way it personifies the area, rising in the uplands of the Brecon Beacons, flowing down through Merthyr Tydfil and the vale beyond, rich in memories of mining, to emerge in the eastern Glamorgan vale close to the sea. It has also given its name to all Welshmen in the somewhat less-than-reverent nickname Taffy. When the A48 is reached at the Taff bridge (162783), a worthwhile excursion is a visit to Llandaff Cathedral. Go up to the A48 and left (SW). The road is crossed using the pedestrian footbridge and a little way SW, beside the rugby club hut, a lane leads off right to Llandaff Cathedral, visible across the playing field of the Cathedral school.

The cathedral itself stands on ground that has been used for Christian worship for 1,400 years. It is likely that the first church here was established by the followers of St. Teilo, one of the greatest of the early British saints. Unusually the 'Llan' – now meaning church, but originally just meaning good land – was not named after the teacher, but after the river. The site is also associated with two other early British bishop/teachers, Dyfrig and Oudoceus, who, together with St. Teilo, have caused three bishop's mitres to be part of the cathedral's coat-of-arms. St. Teilo's legendary visit was around AD 560, but it is doubtful whether a true church was built at that time. Certainly there was a pre-Norman church, the sole surviving piece of which, a Celtic cross, is mounted in the south aisle. The Normans built the first cathedral on the site over a 150-year period from the early twelfth century. Giraldus notes that the site was held in high esteem. This veneration seems to have been due to a number of miraculous events at the site – the ripening of a crop many weeks before time in order to feed the starving of the area at a time of famine; the strange death of a man at exactly the spot he had struck a pilgrim; and others. Part of this church still remains, and of particular interest is that part of the west front between the two towers which is widely thought to be one of the masterpieces of medieval architecture. The northern tower of the west front, known as the Jasper Tower from Jasper Tudor, uncle of Henry VII, who commissioned it, was added, but thereafter the fortunes of the cathedral fell. By the late seventeenth century it was a 'sad and miserable' place, a situation in part due to Cromwell's soldiers who used the nave as a pub and the font as a pig-trough, amongst other indignities. The sad decline was hastened by a storm in 1703 which brought down masonry from the towers, and a further storm 20 years later brought down the south-west tower completely together with much of the roof. Money was raised for restoration and one of the leading architects of the day, John Wood, architect of the Georgian city of Bath, was engaged. His attempt, a classical temple rising from within the ruined walls, attached at points, but leaving some of the original un-roofed ruin, was not held in high esteem. Despite that it remained for 100 years before being dismantled in favour of a complete restoration led by Dean Conybeare. This time there was a local architect, John Pritchard, whose work was an undoubted success. Sadly Conybeare himself did not live to see the completion of the work. His fine memorial can be seen to the south of the cathedral, outside the chapter house. Externally Pritchard's greatest work was the tower and spire on the southern side of the west front. At first glance his work, which at almost 200 feet overtops the medieval Jasper tower and differs in having a spire, destroys the balance of the west front. Further reflection however, and the view of the west front from some way off, particularly from the ruin of the detached Norman belfry on the cathedral green to the south, suggests that such is not the case, the lack of symmetry being a delight. Internally Pritchard made use of the contemporary Pre-Raphaelite artists, Rossetti producing the triptych 'The Seed of David' and Burne-Jones the porcelain panels, 'Six Days of Creation'.

Sadly much of Pritchard's work was destroyed in 1941 when a land-mine was dropped near the cathedral causing severe damage. Indeed only Coventry of Britain's cathedrals was more extensively damaged. Restoration work was started in 1945 and finished finally in 1960. To the northern side of the cathedral were added the David Chapel, a memorial chapel for the Welsh Regiment, and the Processional Way. Most significant, however, was the addition of a large parabolic arch of reinforced concrete between the nave and the choir. The arch supports a concrete cylinder, the organ case adorned by Pre-Raphaelite angels and saints, and supporting also the Sir Jacob Epstein statue 'Christ in Majesty' cast in unpolished aluminium. Again we have a departure from normality, with a clearly modern sculpture mounted on a very modern building material, set in an ancient church. It is clearly a matter of opinion, but the author finds the work and setting superb.

On the hill above the cathedral is the Old Bishop's Palace. It was the largest of several houses that originally stood around the cathedral, and is the only one to have survived. It probably dates from the fourteenth century, but is possibly earlier. A sixteenth-century record refers to it as Llandaff Castle, and such it was, the Norman bishop being a lord of the manor and, as such, able to complete a castle in the same way as other local lords. It was not in use by the time of the record, probably having been made ruinous during the Glyndwr revolt. Entrance to the gardens now enclosed by the walls is by way of the original gatehouse which may have had a drawbridge and certainly had a portcullis protected by arrow slits. Today the gardens are a peaceful place, walls that once protected the insider from marauding hordes now protecting him from the noise and cares of the real world. In this most recent of usages it has been very successful, having won a civic trust award for being 'a positive and valuable asset'.

A little way to the west of Llandaff in the grounds of the castle of St. Fagans is the Welsh Folk Museum, part of the National Museum. The castle is, in reality, an Elizabethan mansion on the

Sir Jacob Epstein's 'Christ in Majesty', Llandaff Cathedral

site of an earlier Norman castle. Within it contains a number of interesting rooms from that period through to more modern times. Outside, the formal gardens lie beside fish-ponds created by damming a small stream and then introducing carp and bream. The formal side of the museum contains exhibitions of agricultural tools and wagons, domestic and cultural life and costume. In the parkland beyond the museum are a number of buildings that have been brought here from various parts of Wales and rebuilt on the site as fine examples of their type.

From Llandaff there is no real alternative to returning to the path beside the Taff at the end of Bute Park. The wayfarer could continue to Llandaff Bridge, to rejoin the Taff there, but this has little merit. At (144793) go diagonally right to the railway bridge. To this point the route has been urban, but here a waterwheel is in the course of reconstruction, and the Melingryffydd factory is an important industrial relic. The road is followed to (144803) where a bridge crosses part of the old Glamorgan canal, now part of a nature reserve. Follow the metalled road on towards Forest Farm. Before the farm, as the road goes right, go straight ahead to a path again beside the river. The route goes under the M4 bridge and on into Tongwynlais.

The history of the iron and steel industry in South Wales will be dealt with more fully when the route reaches Blaenavon, for at that town the history is both continuous and alive in the remains that can still be visited. It was here at Tongwynlais, however, that the industry actually began in South Wales, the first blast furnace being constructed here by iron masters from Sussex in the last third of the sixteenth century.

Now follow the signs to Castell Coch.

Castell Coch

Before the arrival of the M4 motorway that dominates the foreground in any distant view, Castell Coch must have been one of the most picturesque buildings in the whole of Wales. It is for all the world like a Bavarian castle awaiting the arrival of a Wagnerian hero or, as the official Welsh Office guide has it, a fairy-tale castle, a back-cloth for 'Sleeping Beauty'. Interestingly, despite its apparent antiquity it is only a little over 100 years old. The site itself is indeed an ancient one, but the present construction is the work, as at Cardiff Castle, of Lord Bute as patron and William Burges as architect. Bute's requirement was for Burges to reconstruct the original castle and to that end the ruined original was stripped back to the foundations so that Burges could research the design concept. Among other things this showed that the original had been constructed in Old Red Sandstone, explaining the name Castell Coch – Red Castle. From the base Burges then constructed what we see. The conical turrets he added to the completed towers were, he maintained, authentic, pointing to many medieval manuscripts that showed them. He reasoned that a flat roof was only of use if the tower held a war engine, while no roof meant danger during archer attack, for 'if . . . the arrow was fired upright, in its downward flight it might occasion the same accident to the defenders as happened to Harold at Hastings'. What he had failed to point out was that

The Old Bishop's Palace, Llandaff

Castell Coch

manuscripts showing the conical towers were invariably of
European or Oriental origin. It is likely that all this explanation was
tongue in cheek, Burges having cones because he liked them. To
add to this romantic image the cones are all of different sizes and
heights. The castle is entered by bridge and drawbridge through a
gateway fitted with a portcullis, the mechanism for which is
faithfully reproduced inside. Clearly the moat here could not hold
water, but Burges' ideas on drawbridge and portcullis construction
can. Within there is a tiny courtyard, not 20 yards across,
surrounded by roofed galleries reached by staircases. The illusion of
a truly medieval spectacle is lost once the visitor enters the castle
rooms themselves, for here there is a combination of Victorian,
Dark Age and brilliantly individualistic decoration. The Banqueting
Hall has a fine fireplace adorned with a statue of St. Lucius, the

legendary King of Britain in the early years of the third century. The wall murals are of episodes from the lives of martyrs.

The Drawing Room is an astonishing place. Burges maintained that he had 'ventured to indulge in a little more ornament'. He was clearly not given to understatement as there appears to be no square inch of wall surface without decoration. The decoration is thematic: the lower walls have panels representing different plants; around the doors the wildlife theme is continued, with the life-history of birds and butterflies together with mice and snails; the walls depict scenes from Aesop's Fables; there are the zodiacal signs and figures from Greek mythology; the ceilings are birds and butterflies against a back-drop of star-lit sky. By contrast the three heraldic shields are almost plain. After the Drawing Room the Bedrooms appear plain and somewhat lacking in imagination, but the windlass room that contains the drive for the portcullis has interest. Here imagination is revived, Burges having provided 'sundry holes in the floor and a fireplace in order to heat water and other substances to pour down on the enemy'. Thankfully the only horde to have breached the castle's outer defences is that of the summer visitors. Externally the castle is well worth a walk-around. It is likely that despite the extravagance of the interior and the conical turrets, the castle is a reasonable replica of a small early Norman castle. The first builders certainly had an eye for position, the castle being excellently sited to protect the narrow gorge of the Taff before it spread out into the coastal plain.

From the castle the route follows the obvious track, north-east then north, through a beautiful piece of woodland to emerge on the minor road at (143840). Go right and immediately take a lane left through trees that leads to another minor road at (145838). Go across and take the well marked and distinct bridleway to Thornhill (158845). Cross the A469 with care and go north along it to a gate on the right labelled 'Wide View'.

A little to the south from here is Castell Morgraig, a Welsh castle from the thirteenth century probably started by the lord of Senghenydd whose lands were confiscated. Because, for that reason, it was never finished what remains is a true building record, the castle never having been attacked or slighted. Beyond is Cefn

Onn, the name being given also to the country park a little below
the southern ridge crest. This is another of Cardiff's wide range of
parks, Cefn Onn being a fine place in springtime when the
rhododendrons bloom.

The bridleway leads to Cefn Onn Farm (182856).

A little over a mile to the north-west at this point, in the
Rhymney valley at the base of the escarpment, there is, at
Caerphilly, a town famous for its cheese and the castle, one of the
largest fortified castles in Europe. For the visitor interested in 'real'
castles this site coming soon after the Burges works at Cardiff and
Castell Coch is a blessing – the castle is functional rather than
decorative. Interestingly Caerphilly also owes its existence, in such a
good state of repair, to the third Lord Bute.

Early work was concentrated on this site as it represented the
approximate boundary between Norman Glamorgan and the Wales
of the princes of Wales, but it was made redundant by the wars of
Edward I. As a result of its part in several murderous royal disputes
the castle gained a black reputation recalled by a Welsh poet's wish
that a dead enemy's soul 'may go to Caerphilly'. The castle was
briefly held by Owain Glyndwr in the fifteenth century, but was
then abandoned completely until the Civil War when it was slighted,
possibly to prevent its use as a fortification, possibly to learn more
of the potential power of gunpowder on masonry. The cleaved, and
leaning, south-east tower bears witness to the considerable power of
the new weapon. The tower is, in fact, only 10 degrees from the
vertical, but its disjointed nature makes it appear to lean much
more.

The site covers 30 acres and the castle was the first concentric
design in Britain. The defences are a complex and powerful
combination of water and masonry. Those who have the time
should visit the site. Due to its position, a little too close to the
mining valleys and too far from the sea, the castle has never really
gained the reputation it deserves when compared to the
contemporary sites of the north – Caernarfon, Conwy, Harlech,
Beaumaris. It is worth a detour to measure up an impression against
Tennyson's, who exclaimed 'It isn't a castle, it's a whole ruined
town!'

Leave the farm on its southern side and follow a pathway which is more distinct in the forest, and leads to the doorway of the *Maenllwyd Inn* (201866). The metalled lane to the east of the pub, running north-east, is followed. Where the lane swings left and upwards towards Penrhow Farm go through a gate, right, (208871) to a bridleway in the forest. This is followed, dog-legging at (213873), to a minor road. Turn left and follow the road to Machen.

Machen

Machen is a strange town divided into two. The lower village, now called Lower Machen though originally called Chatham after an early inhabitant, is a country village that would not appear out-of-place if it were plucked from its site and set down in any of a dozen locations in England. The church at its heart is very English with its squat, castellated tower. It was reputedly founded in the sixth century, but the present building is an amalgam of pieces from the twelfth to the fifteenth centuries. There is a sundial above the porch, and the south wall of the tower has a slab incised with a Gorgon-like face with huge staring eyes but, sadly, no inscription. This was long thought to have been brought here from a pagan altar, but it is generally agreed now that the stylised nature of the work makes it more likely to have been a decoration piece by a medieval mason. John Wesley preached here in 1741, in English, to a vast crowd who, if they gathered in the churchyard, probably upset the woonts. These were such a nuisance that the churchwarden's records of 1772 note that a payment was made of 3 shillings to a parishioner for 'kotching woonts'. The problem appears to have been the considerable number of woonta-tomps that the creatures (also known as moles) pushed up.

Between the villages, on the south-eastern flank of Mynydd Machen, is Castell Meredydd, built in the early thirteenth century by a descendant of Hywel Dda. It is in a very ruinous state, for after being captured by the Normans in 1236 it appears to have been abandoned and allowed to decay.

The upper village is less picturesque, although it too has a fine church set in a leafy churchyard with, at the right time of year, a noisy rookery. Special mention must be made of the spire that

emerges from the roof off-centre, like a chimney. Equally
interesting is the village pub which is called the *Fwrrwm Ishta*. Since
the initial 'f' is pronounced as 'f', rather than as 'v', it should strictly
be 'ff' which is the Welsh letter 'f'. It would then read Ffwrrwm
which means, pedantically, that it starts with four double letters,
which must be a record of some sort.

In earlier times Machen was the centre of the local flannel
industry, a number of fulling mills being built along the Rhymney
river. The flannel was also dyed here, in two colours only – red or
grey. The red flannel was more expensive because it was better for
curing chest colds, a notion that may be more to do with some not
understood herbal effect of the red dye than pure supposition. The
industry did not survive the opening up of newer mills elsewhere,
because the Rhymney had a habit of running very low in summer
which meant no power for the water wheels. This lack of continuous
torrents may also explain the will of an inhabitant who granted land
to the Baptist church on a lease that should be for 'as long as there
remains a stone in Rhymney river'.

To leave Machen take the road opposite the *Fwrrwm Ishta*, and
just beyond the church take the footpath off right which goes
through the forest and out onto Mynydd Machen. There is no path
to the summit, but the top is worth the visit. It is the first top on the
route, an important landmark therefore, and has good views into
the valleys. To the north of the park there are tracks down through
the forest, but the wayfarer may also follow the road from the radio
masts that is joined at (223906). The road falls quickly down
through the forest to the Ebbw river and Black Vein Road in Risca.

Risca

For those exploring South Wales for the first time using the route
described here Risca is the first contact with a Welsh mining valley
and the landscape and community made famous over the years by
romantic allusions such as *How Green was my Valley*. At Machen
the terraced nature of the valley housing has been seen, but it is at
Risca that the force of the nineteenth-century industrialisation
becomes apparent. One of the first signs of approach to the mining
heartland is the river crossed by the wayfarer on his way from

Mynydd Machen to the town, for this is the Ebbw river. In the upper reaches it is two streams, the Ebbw Fach flowing down from beneath Brynmawr to meet the Ebbw Fawr, which has risen near Ebbw Vale itself. The combined streams then join the Sirhowy river that has cut the next valley to the west, with Tredegar at its head, at Crosskeys a mile to the west of Risca itself. The journey from Rogerstone, a couple of miles to the east of Risca, to Newbridge 5 miles up the Ebbw valley assures the traveller of the full flavour of South Wales with its power station, winding engines, chapels and terraces.

The first thing that strikes the newcomer to this spot on the Ebbw is not the industrialisation, but the clarity of the water and the beauty of the river. It is a sad truth that the visitor expects to find a grimy river and is surprised that it still exhibits the beauty that all of these steep-sided valleys must have had at some stage in the Middle Ages.

The history of coalmining in the area goes back beyond the Middle Ages, for the Romans knew of the coal. They had established a legionary fort at Isca, as they called Caerleon, about 6 miles to the east of Risca. In the area around Mynydd Machen they dug for galena, the mineral that yields lead and some silver, and probably took coal that was easily available. It was not until the early thirteenth century that any great interest was taken in coal, when its usefulness was discovered by blacksmiths and limeburners, making agricultural lime, and, in limited quantities, by the locals for domestic use. The area shows many depressions left by the partial filling of bell-pits, as the earliest mines were called. Here a single vertical shaft was dug until the coal seam was hit, and the miner then worked horizontally outwards along the seam producing an excavation that resembled a handbell. Since seams that were close to the surface were at a premium many bell-pits were dug, the primary skill of the miner being in deciding how close he could dig to the next pit before the unsupported ground above collapsed. It was a dangerous occupation, and hard work as the coal, and the miners of course, had to be brought up by means of windlasses erected over the shafts and driven by muscle-power.

Historical reviews of the valleys stress the importance of

coalmining and it is difficult to realise that the coal industry was, in fact, a subsidiary industry to several others (but chiefly ironmaking) until little over a century ago. In Risca the chief industry when the town began to emerge as such was brick making. In 1747 John Wesley visited the valley on a conversion crusade and noted Risca as 'a pleasant village at the foot of the hills'. At that time it was, largely, an agriculturally based community, but the land was different in one respect from that of surrounding towns. There was little iron-stone, so important to the development of Blaenavon as we shall see later, but there was clay in abundance, clay for house bricks and clay for fire bricks. During the second quarter of the nineteenth century Risca therefore became the centre for the brick industry in South Wales. Over the course of the next hundred years numerous extensive sites arose along the river and the canal. The canal itself was an arm of the Monmouthshire canal that extended from Brynglas in Newport to Crumlin in the Ebbw valley above Newbridge. The Darren brickworks, the first to be constructed, produced over one million bricks in the first four years of its process, and with the exception of one, owned by the inappropriately named Fergus Brain, all the works were a resounding success. To heat their kilns the brickwork owners used local coal. In the last two decades of the eighteenth century coal had been mined in the area by a company owned by children of Charles Phillips, the local squire. Phillips was one of the larger-than-life people that the British are renowned for producing, a giant of a man standing 6 feet 4 inches. He was famous as a hunting man and once presented 12 pairs of his own hounds to George III at Windsor. Once while out hunting he wagered that he could jump a canal lock on horseback. Apparently he almost made it, landing head first on the far side. For his failure he not only lost his bet, but spent the rest of his life with a metal plate in his head. It appears that eight children were involved in the coalmining venture, a great number you might think, but only a small fraction of the total, as Phillips could call on 26 in all.

By this time the shafts to the coal seams were deeper than those of the bell-pit and the windlass had to be replaced by a more efficient lifting machine. At the early Risca works the machine used was the Whimsey. The easiest, and perhaps least scientific, way of describing the device is to say it was a hamster's exercise wheel, with the hamster replaced by a horse and a winding rope wound around the central shaft. When steam power became available, the more recognisable winding machine was used. These developments followed developments in the industry itself, which came in the first half of the nineteenth century. At that stage coal, which had been a subsidiary industry – indeed at Risca some coal production was a byproduct of claymining – became a major industry. The chief reasons were the discovery of the use of coke in iron smelting, the invention and development of the steam engine and railways, and domestic usage as fuel. Before 1840 it is estimated that a total of about 1.5 million tons of coal had been mined in the Welsh valleys. In the single year of 1874 over 16 million tons were mined. By the outbreak of war in 1914 a quarter of a million men were employed in the mines.

The history of Welsh coalmining is a story of many individuals, the most famous perhaps being David Davies of Llandinam in Montgomeryshire who opened up the Rhondda valley. His is the archetypal story, perhaps more myth than fact, of being down to his last half-crown when he had paid off his men for the last time. With a flamboyant gesture he gave them that as well and they were so impressed that they worked for one last time on the shafts and discovered the richest of the Rhondda seams – or so the story goes.

The mines exploited by the early entrepreneurs were dangerous, with continuous high risks from water and gas. The water risk was lessened, though water remained an economic problem, by wheel-driven pumps, but gas could never be really overcome. Forced ventilation by building furnaces under 'up-shafts' and so drawing clean air from 'down-shafts' through the mines was reasonably successful, but it was the Davy lamp that finally offered some means of security. The introduction of the lamp was, initially, not a success as the light from it was poor in comparison to that from a candle, and the men preferred the candle despite the risk of igniting the firedamp. In 1860 at the Blackvein works 142 men and boys were killed in a single explosion. Of the victims 22 were under 15 and a further 24 under 20. After the disaster the report in *The*

Times revealed the (slowly) changing attitude of the establishment to the colliers. Before that time all such disasters were seen in purely financial, i.e. owner-biased, terms. The reporter at Risca wrote, 'I am utterly at a loss to understand how any man can be got to follow a calling which, of all others by which men earn their bread, is the most disagreeable, the most laborious, and a hundred-fold more perilous. The winter will bring misery and privations to many a hearth.' The report overlooks the way in which the pits had been worked in earlier times – by fear, fear of lost wages and lost jobs. The birth of unionism in the valleys had been strongly opposed by the owners. There had been riots, often quelled by troops. In one uprising at Merthyr the commander of the troops dispersed an ugly crowd by having one of his men slice a dog in half to demonstrate his ability to handle a weapon.

Better conditions came eventually, but slowly, and largely as the result of the increase in demand for coal. Following the First World War, however, the coal industry went into a decline and all the Risca collieries have now ceased operation. Gone too are the metal works, copper and steel, the valley having become largely silent again. The town is architecturally interesting to those who study the ribbon development of the valleys, but has a uniformity which does not have mass appeal. The church, to St. Mary, was built in 1852 on the site of an older building that may even have been Norman.

In the main, however, the religion of the town, as of the area, was, and is, Nonconformist. These churches accompanied the workers who came to the area from rural Wales and England in the wake of the industrial expansion, maintaining faith with the people at a time when the Anglican clergy was supporting the establishment, the mine owners and ironmasters. Any visitor to Risca should therefore note the bold lines of the many chapels.

Black Vein Road is followed to the A467. Go right and just before the Risca town sign go left up Medart Street. At the end of the street follow the footpath and canal pathway to the lane at (234915). Go north to Hanson's Lodge (236925) and through Ebbw forest to Mynydd Henllys at (248934). Here the walker has reached the terrain he came in search of, for this is very fine fell walking, even if the views are less expansive and less spectacular

Two studies in Nonconformity – Moriah Baptist Chapel (above) and Trinity Methodist Chapel (right), Risca

than those farther north. The summit of the ridge Mynydd Maen, is as open as many that will follow, our route going above the aptly named *Mountain Air Inn* at (277979) to join the road near the *Lamb Inn* at (282991). Go round north of the inn and follow the semi-metalled lane down into Pontypool.

Pontypool
To look at Pontypool now it is difficult to believe that it is a very recent town. When Llantarnam Abbey, near the Afon Llwyd, south of Cwmbran, was founded at the end of the twelfth century lands in the valley of the Llwyd were conferred on it. It would be of great interest to travel back to that time and see the valley as it then was, devoid of the effects of industrialisation.

At that time there appears to have been no village here at all,

although the river valleys were farmed, so there may have been isolated farms or a hamlet in the area. The name of the town derives from a bridge over the river which was placed here certainly by the early sixteenth century. Legend has it that a local parson David, son of Howel, met the Devil at the river's edge one night after a particularly good supper. Since David enjoyed the odd glass of ale, or two, he was in good spirits and readily agreed to a tug of war over the water, the loser to build a bridge. This is a novel twist to Devil stories, where Nick takes his winnings in souls, but the outcome was the usual one with David winning. Next day there was a new stone bridge over the water which the parson named after his father, Pont-ap-Howel. It is more likely that the 'pool' was an Anglican appendage to the Welsh pont, to signify its position near boggy ground at the water margin. Interestingly though, the oldest part of the village is called Pontymoel to this day.

As early as 1425 there was a forge in the area run by cousins from Trevethin. They had several small forges and were known by the Welsh name gof, or smith, a name they later used as a surname, changing the spelling to Gough, although keeping the pronounciation. Why the spelling should have changed is a mystery. The Goughs' ironworks continued for almost 150 years, then they were taken over by one of the groups of Sussex ironmasters moving into the area in the late sixteenth century. Shortly after this the most significant event in the history of the town took place, for in 1576 the Earl of Pembroke, Lord of Usk, leased land, including all iron and coal workings, in the Pontypool area of the Llwyd valley to a partnership containing one Richard Hanbury, a goldsmith of London. The rent was one guinea and 32 oxen annually, with Pembroke having the right to ask for £2 for every ox he felt unworthy. The partnership had made a very good deal. The association of Hanbury and Pontypool was long-lasting and fruitful, one of the fruits being borne away to the USA where in Massachusetts the first adventurers from this country who were skilled in forge iron manufacture were two brothers James and Henry Leonard. They went to Bristol county, Massachusetts, in 1652, from Pontypool, and built the first forge in America.

Richard Hanbury was what could best be described as a rogue.

He chopped down trees he was not entitled to take and refused to pay the fines imposed on him, and he broke contracts he had with the Tintern ironworks, by diverting good quality iron for private sale, 'to his own lucre and gain' as the wire-work masters so beautifully put it. For this he was summoned by the Privy Council as he was seriously jeopardising the wire-works' continued survival. It was clearly a major offence as he was told to pay £100 annually for 9 years and to deliver 15 tons of good iron immediately. This was a very large fine, but by then Hanbury was hugely rich. He used his wealth to his own, good, advantage and to the prosperity of his works by buying up remaining forests when wood was becoming increasingly scarce and by building ships to carry the iron all over Britain. By the time of his death in 1608, the works around Pontypool were of considerable importance. The works and lands that Hanbury owned passed to his nephews and through them to Major John Hanbury, a lawyer who gave up practice in order to concentrate on iron, and money, making. By the late seventeenth century the works were profitable enough to allow certain experimentation to take place. The first innovation was in 1682 when Thomas Cooke was brought down from Stonebridge and succeeded in not only raising the general level of mechanisation but in producing the first rolling mill. The patent for this was not actually granted until 1728, for 'expanding bars by the means of compressing cylinders'. The original cylinders were operated by waterwheel, both upper and lower rollers moving to produce good quality plate in large quantities. With the plate Hanbury made saucepans and kettles all at about one-third of the cost of the normal wares, cornering the market and producing considerable profits. Following the production of plate iron experiments were carried out in the tinning of the plates using Cornish tin. By 1720 success had been achieved and a tinplate industry was started in the town. Such was the expertise here that a tinplate works set up in Worcestershire had first to pay £36. 15s. for 'information in tinning' to the Pontypool owners.

   Later again, the work of Thomas Allgood, a Northamptonshire man, employed by the Hanbury family to manage the Pontymoel works, led to the production of Pontypool Japan ware. Allgood discovered that varnishes extracted from coal allowed him to produce a lacquer that would give thin iron plate a very hard shell with good colour and an excellent smooth surface. The plate produced was called Japan ware because of its similarity to Japanese lacquering. Later there were many makers of Japan ware, but that from Pontypool remained the most prized, the colours being particularly brilliant, and the lacquer being heat-resistant allowing kettles to be made as well as the standard trays and tea caddies. The actual recipe of the varnish and the lacquering technique remained a closely guarded secret. The best work produced by the local works dates from the last 20 years of the eighteenth century when the tinplate produced here was of very high quality. The background colour of the ware was invariably black, and this perfectly set off the designs among which butterflies figure strongly.

A fine feature of the town is the park at its heart. This also allows the visitor to take a traffic-free walk and see some of the better sites in the town. Just over the bridge from the car park, near the leisure centre, to the right of the path, is the site of Richard Hanbury's first forge. The remains were here until the early nineteenth century when a later member of the family removed them. Up river another bridge and pathway leads to the town's main street, Hanbury Road, near to the Town Hall, a building in the grand style from 1850, and St. James' church, a very modern building compared with the old church at Trevethin. North of the bridge is Pontypool Park House, home of the Hanbury family. The frontage dates from around 1700, but most of the house is later, building work having been carried on for about 150 years by various members of the family. It is a fine building, but equally fine are the stables next door built in late Georgian style with an elegant archway leading to a cobbled square. The stable block now houses The Valley Inheritance, a museum to the industrial history of the Llwyd valley. The site is an interesting one, the museum also owning other buildings of historical interest including the ironworks and Big Pit colliery at Blaenavon. Opposite the stables there is a small brick-built ice store. Here ice, from the ponds in the winter, brought in by rail in summer, would be laid between layers of straw to produce a refrigerator.

The Hanbury's house, Pontypool Park

Returning now towards the leisure centre the wayfarer passes a shrine to the Welsh national game. This was the home ground of the legendary Pontypool front row, the threesome also providing Wales with one of its best ever front rows. The magnificence of the Arms Park stadium in Cardiff and the simplicity of this site characterise the game in Wales, at one level a game for people to enjoy, at another a national pride. Exit from the park is made at a pair of elaborate gates (291006) erected in 1835 when the whole park was still in Hanbury hands. From there take the pathway north. This pathway can also be reached by going through the park to its northern edge and exiting on the track that leaves it there. From here to Blorenge mountain the route is easy to follow being distinct in the earlier stages and, though indistinct, lying on open moorland in the later stages. The ridge walk here is excellent, with fine views to the valleys and an improving view ahead. The 'real' mountains of

Wales are tantalisingly close now, and though glimpses can be caught of them the wayfarer has to wait until Blorenge is reached for the view to open up fully. A minor road is reached at (277077) which the walker can follow to Blaenavon to glimpse there, at first hand, the history of the valleys before embarking on his high-level passage through Wales. If he is eager to start he can continue directly to the WT station.

Blaenavon

While the romance of the industrialised valleys of South Wales is, for the layman, clearly associated with the Rhondda valley and the Ebbw Vale, it is doubtful whether a single town characterises the area better than Blaenavon, both in the geographic sense and in terms of industrial archaeology. The valley town of legend clings in terraced ranks to a steep hillside, the winding gear of the pit dominating some part of the scene. Blaenavon has its winding gear, though it is some way from the town, and its terraced ranks, though the valley side is not steep. Additionally it has the bleak upland that characterised the area before the industrialisation of the valleys, and an enviable place in the history of that industrialisation.

The town is situated at the head of the valley of the Afon Llwyd, and named after that situation. It was not set there for any reason associated with the river, but because of the existence of ironstone deposits below the moorland immediately to the north and north-west of the town. The Welsh ironstone band stretched from here to Hirwaun, some 18 miles, and yielded an ore that could have an iron content of up to 40 per cent in the 'Black Band' ironstones, so called because of the distinctive colouration the high iron content gave the ore. There was an iron industry from earliest times in Wales, but this was forge-based rather than furnace-based. As has been noted, there was such a forge in Pontypool as early as 1425. By the close of the fifteenth century blast furnaces were in operation in Sussex. By the latter half of the sixteenth century, however, the Sussex industry had been stopped by Act of Parliament. The reasons for this are not clear. It has been argued that the need for charcoal to fire the furnaces, 16 tons of wood being required to produce 1 ton of iron, had denuded the great forests of Southern England and in consequence the Admiralty was concerned for the ship-building industry. Since different woods were used in the two industries this cannot be the whole story, but whatever the reason the ironmasters were in need of new sites. In south Glamorgan they found what they required. Here there were forests in plenty on the sides of valleys whose streams were powerful enough to drive waterwheels which in turn drove bellows to produce the blast. Favourable conditions were found at a number of sites, several of which were in the valley of the Llwyd which had the Blaenavon ironstone as an addition to the required wood and water. Initially the sites were in the lower valley around Pontypool where the stream was broad and strong. Ironstone and also coal were obtained at the time by 'scouring', a curious extraction process made possible by the proximity of the mineral beds to the ground surface. Initially the turf and top soil would be loosened over a patch of land, and then streams above the land would be dammed to form a lake. When sufficient water had accumulated the dam was broken and the water scoured away the top soil leaving the mineral beds bare and ready for working. Not surprisingly this procedure has had a lasting effect on the area of moorland above the town. It may also explain why the stream is known as Afon Llwyd, the grey river. Certainly its appearance now, crystal clear, belies the name, but originally scouring took place on six days each week and would certainly have made the river muddy. Inevitably pieces of ironstone and coal were caught up in the scour water and carried downstream, where the old and poor of the lower valley scratched a living by collecting the ironstone and gaining some comfort from the coal each winter. Under Cromwell this practice came to the notice of the Exchequer who promptly taxed the gatherers. The tax was short-lived, however, the valley folk deciding they would rather stop collecting than pay it.

Eventually the forests of the lower valleys were also denuded, and the outlook would have been very black but for the discovery, in the first half of the eighteenth century, of the use of coke as an alternative fuel for the smelting of iron. Now Blaenavon came into its own for on the one site there was now coal suitable for coking, iron ore, building stone and water. Additionally there was limestone which was used as a flux in the furnace. In 1789 the first ironworks was built by Thomas Hill of Stafford with Benjamin Pratt of Worcestershire and Welshman Thomas Hopkins. The site is of such interest that it has now been taken into the care of the Welsh Office and is being refurbished as a museum of the iron industry. Investigation of the site reveals that there were five furnaces built into the hillside so that they could be charged directly from above. Also on the site are the remains of the balance tower. Here water was piped into a box until it was heavy enough to lift a trolley loaded with pig iron from the casting floor level up to 'moor' level and transportation. At the base the water was emptied and the water box was lifted back to the tower top by the weight of the descending pig trolley. Near the ironworks themselves is a small square that once housed some of the workers. One side of the square is open on to the site itself. The two parallel sides contain the two-up, two-down cottages of craftsmen and their families, while the back row was the works offices on the ground floor and a dormitory for labourers above. The houses are also to be restored, but it is even now possible to visit them. It is difficult to believe that in one of these tiny cottages one man, or more specifically his wife, raised 19 children. Clearly the workers of the day, the late eighteenth to early nineteenth centuries, did not enjoy a quality lifestyle. Since the square also contained the only Blaenavon shop at the time, and that run by the company, neither did they enjoy much quantity. The obvious difference between the ironmasters and the workers, as exemplified for instance by the difference between the houses near the ironworks and Ty Mawr built at an early point by Thomas Hill, led to considerable anger. The men were forbidden to join a union, but an employers' association existed to ensure that profits were maximised and wages minimised. It is, perhaps, worth noting here that the slang word 'screw' for a prison warder originated at this time. It was not only an offence for a man to join a union but also to strike, the latter being punishable by three months' hard labour at the Usk prison where the prisoners enjoyed the hard boredom of the treadmill. The 'screw' was the warder who tightened up the screw on the treadmill shaft to increase the labour required. With iron in demand during the Napoleonic wars the grievances of the men simmered, but following the end of the war in 1815 there was an iron slump and wages were cut savagely to keep profits up. The men revolted and 10,000 from Merthyr, Tredegar and Blaenavon went on strike with the slogan 'Bread or Blood', a true sign of despair. Troops were called in, but the ironmasters gave in and wages were restored. The peace was short-lived, however, and for two decades trouble flared intermittently and violently. The history of nonconformity in South Wales was fostered at this time with the nonconformist ministers keeping faith with their flock while the church ministers, especially the Rev. William Powell of Abergavenny, tended to side with the ironmasters. Powell was a magistrate as well as a rector, and in that capacity called in troops on occasion to put down strikes and riots, as well as planting spies among the men to obtain a little prior knowledge. He was also enthusiastic that the troops should be under the control of the magistrates fearing, rightly, that the officers were more sympathetic to the men's cause.

Perhaps to respond to the influence of the nonconformists the ironmasters, Hill and Hopkins, built St. Peter's church in 1805. It is a simple local stone structure with a considerable quantity of cast iron work that makes it most interesting. Window frames and sills, and tomb covers are of iron, as is the font, a feature which is unique. In addition to the church the ironmasters did raise some public buildings. Most notable is St. Peter's School built as a memorial to Samuel Hopkins, the son of Thomas, by his sister Sarah in 1815. The Latin inscription, when translated, notes that the school carried into effect 'the benevolent intentions of her deeply lamented and most deserving brother towards his Blenavonians'. Hopkins' intentions could be argued, but the last word is clearly a spelling mistake, probably by a cutter who did not know Blaenavon well.

In 1860 a new works was opened on the other side of the Afon Llwyd. The stage was then set for the revolution in metal making that was to take place in Blaenavon. In 1856 the work of Bessemer and Siemens had allowed steel to replace iron as the primary constructional metal. However the processes could only produce good quality steel, that is metal not susceptible to brittle fracture,

from low phosphorus ores which constituted only 10 per cent of all
known deposits. The problem of how to remove phosphorus from
normal ores was unsolved, and apparently insoluble, for 20 years
until experiments at Blaenavon showed the way. The experiments
were carried out by Sidney Gilchrist Thomas, not a chemist or even
someone employed at Blaenavon. He was, in fact, a clerk at the
Metropolitan Police Courts, a situation forced upon him by the
need to be a wage-earner following the early, and sudden, death of
his father. Thomas was a keen amateur chemist and was obsessed by
the problem of phosphoric steels. His early work was carried out in
his rooms where he built a small furnace, but this was not successful
and once he set the rooms alight. The turning point came in 1876
when his cousin, Percy Gilchrist, was appointed Chemist at
Blaenavon. From then on Thomas lived a hectic life travelling to
Blaenavon at the weekends to carry out experiments on the plant.
The company manager, when he discovered the, initially,
clandestine operations, was enthusiastic and by 1878 Thomas and
his cousin had achieved the breakthrough. The essence of the
solution to the problem that Thomas had devised was the use of a
basic (in the chemical sense) rather than a siliceous furnace lining,
producing a basic slag rather than an acid slag. Not only had
Thomas solved the problem but he realised that the resulting slag,
rich in phosphorus, would be extremely valuable in agriculture as a
fertiliser.

Following the announcement in 1879 of the discovery, Thomas
was feted in all the steelmaking countries of the world and travelled
extensively to secure patents and meet ironmasters. Andrew
Carnegie, the famous Scottish-American industrialist, became his
friend and invited him to America. He was obviously very
impressed with the discovery declaring, 'These two young men,
Thomas and Gilchrist of Blaenavon, did more for Britain's
greatness than all the Kings and Queens put together. Moses struck
the rock and brought forth water. They struck the useless
phosphoric ore and transformed it into steel – a far greater miracle.'
He was equally impressed with Thomas maintaining, 'He had only
to appear and we bowed before his power'. Sadly, however, the
hectic pre-discovery life involving endless travelling, poor diet and

little sleep took its toll on Thomas and he became very ill. Despite this he continued to travel and meet ironmasters growing weaker with every journey. Finally, in 1885, at the young age of 35 he died in Paris. In Britain Thomas never received the recognition he deserved. Abroad the best steels are Thomas steels, and the agricultural slag is known as Thomas slag. There is some evidence of change now and, most fittingly, a fine memorial has been raised at the site of the second ironworks, to the east of the Llwyd, where the cousins carried out their tests.

In the wake of the discovery a new company was formed at Blaenavon but the difficulty in obtaining ore meant that steel production finally stopped in the town in 1938. More recently the site of the new ironworks has been taken over by a new metal-working company producing and working special alloys, chiefly for the aerospace industries.

The most tangible reminder of the Blaenavon steel industry is the Workmen's Hall and Institute. This was opened in 1894 with steelworkers and miners paying weekly contributions to pay off mortgages taken on their houses by some of the founders. Many such buildings were raised in the valleys at that time, but this at Blaenavon is, arguably, the finest one ever built. At the outset it was decided that the building should house a library, paid for and maintained by the community for half a century until the County Council took it over. The building is a tribute to the men who built it.

From earliest times, and particularly after the discovery of iron smelting by coke fuel, Blaenavon had a coal industry. In 1840 when a Parliamentary Commission was set up to investigate conditions in mines they visited Blaenavon, and what they found there led directly to the Mines Act of 1842. In the pits they found women stripped to the waist hauling coal trams and young children performing critical functions underground for many hours alone each day. This latter use of children often led to appalling accidents when they were left in charge of machinery, on occasions even the winding gear. The Commission found a boy of seven already a vereran of three years in the mine, who smoked a pipe all day in order to stay awake, and a girl not quite seven who was asleep in

The winding engine, Big Pit, Blaenavon

pitch darkness. Her lamp had gone out and the rats had eaten her
lunch and so she had gone to sleep alone in the dark. She was lucky,
she had been in the pit only 15 months. The Commission reported
to Parliament noting that in 1838, the latest year when complete
records were available, there had been, throughout British mines,
58 deaths of children under 13 and 62 more of children from 13 to
18. Now, 150 years removed from the Commission's report, it is
obvious to us that the whole of Parliament would be appalled by
these facts. It was not, some members claiming that to ban children
from the mines would bring about the collapse of the industry.
Nevertheless the Mines Act was passed forbidding women and girls,
and boys under ten, to work underground. It was opposed by both
the families, who needed the money, and the mine owners, who
wanted the higher profits available from using cheaper labour. In
consequence the law was ignored, and inspectors of mines were
appointed in 1850 to ensure compliance. The first inspector at
Blaenavon turned out 70 women and children and was promptly
besieged by the women angry at their loss of income. It took several
years for the practice to die completely.

The last working pit in Blaenavon, Big Pit to the north-east of the
town, closed recently. It was one of the oldest shaft pits in South
Wales with galleries dating from the very early nineteenth century.
Immediately it was closed it was taken over for refurbishment as a
mining museum. The project, one of the most imaginative to be
undertaken in Wales, is long term, but already tours of the
above-ground buildings are available to tourists and it is hoped that
in the near future visitors will be able to go underground.

Little remains on the moorland to the north-east of Blaenavon as
a memorial to the town's industrial past, a situation very different
from that which exists to the north-west of the town where a jumble
of open-cast mines and scourings now even obliterate the route
taken by the tramways down to the works. To the west of the radio
masts, however, the Penffordd-goch pond is a reminder of the
industrial past. The pond is not natural, though the years have
softened the artificial edges and given it a 'real' look. It was
constructed to supply the forge at Garnddyris a little way north, and
down the hill.

FOXHUNTER
23rd April 1940 – 21st November 1959

Here lies FOXHUNTER
Champion International Show Jumper

Winner of 78 International Competitions
including many foreign Grand Prix
and the
King George V Gold Cup. 1948. 1950 and 1953.

35 times member of the British Show
Jumping Team which won
Olympic Gold Medals at Helsinki 1952.
Bronze Medals at London. 1948.
Prince of Wales Cup, London,
five times (1949-1953) and the
Aga Khan Cup outright,
Dublin (1950, 1951-1953)

Foxhunter's memorial, Blorenge Mountain

Whether the wayfarer has gone directly to the WT station, or gone via Blaenavon, he will now be opposite the Foxhunter car park. The car park takes its name from the show-jumper Foxhunter who is buried among the rocks at its northern end. The horse was owned by Col. Harry Llewellyn of Govilon, and a memorial plaque also set among the rocks recalls the horse and rider's fine achievements, which included a gold medal at the Helsinki Olympic Games of 1952.

From the car park the choice of route is governed by questions of right of way and by personal preference. Those wishing to avoid the suggested horseshoe route on the Black Mountains can go westward past Penffordd-goch pond and across the lunar landscape to the top of the Clydach gorge at (216123) from where steps descend the gorge. The A465 is negotiated by subway to the minor road for Blackrock. Go right through the quarry to arrive on the Llangattock escarpment road at (218130) and follow it to the kilns at Darren Cilau (205153). Since, as mentioned below, the traverse of Mynydd Llangynydr is not on a right of way, some may prefer to descend to the Brecon and Monmouthshire canal and to follow its towpath to Llangynydr. This route will be mentioned more fully below.

The descent to Llanfoist is, however, in itself ambiguous. Signs at the car park tell the wayfarer how to ascend Blorenge mountain though this is not on a right of way, and publications of the Brecon Beacons National Park include walks from Llanfoist to Blorenge even though the routes are not on rights of way. To add to the complication the descent route to Llanfoist is quite clearly signed, at Llanfoist church, as a public footpath to Blorenge.

The view from Blorenge summit is quite superb, with the Usk valley below and a backdrop of the Black Mountains and Sugar Loaf. The descent is made north-east to Little Pen-y-Craig cottage at (282127) from where a steeply descending path goes under the canal to Llanfoist.

The canal is now called the Brecon and Monmouthshire though when constructed it was the Brecon and Abergavenny, the Monmouthshire then being a separate canal. These canals were built in what can be termed the golden age of canal construction, the last decade of the eighteenth century. The era of canals was short, as the arrival of the railways curtailed building in the first half of the nineteenth century, but intensive.

As a contrast to the majority of canals the Brecon and Abergavenny was primarily non-industrial, having been built to carry coal to Brecon and to carry lime to the farmers and other farm produce back to the markets. As with all other canals it required a company to raise capital for its construction, to survey the route and to arrive at agreements with landowners, and it required an Act of Parliament to allow construction. The proposed canal was 33 miles long, from Brecon to the already approved Monmouthshire canal at Pontymoel near Pontypool. The Act received Royal assent in 1793 and work began the following year. The Act enabled the canal company to build tramroads up to eight miles distant from the canal itself, this concession being termed the 'mileage' in all canal costs, and this was of great value to the companies as it allowed them to

The Monmouthshire and Brecon Canal, Llanfoist

offer a service to many industries along its route. The normal
method of business was for the canal company to construct the
tramroad and buy the rolling stock and then to levy the company for
its use. Any private owner of a tram could also use the road, upon
payment of a fee, though this offer was infrequently taken up as the
cost of vehicles was high. The tramway concession explains why
early construction concentrated on tramway construction, the canal
itself being started only in 1797. Probably because of the lack of
significant waterside industries the canal company ran into financial
difficulties which several times halted construction, and it was not
until 1812 that the canal was finally completed. Though this was
considered at the time to be a long time, and does appear excessive,
15 years for 33 miles, it has to be remembered that the canal was
hand dug by 'navvies', the short form of navigators as the men were
called who dug these navigations. Their only mechanical devices

were the pickaxe, the shovel and the wheelbarrow. There was also a significant amount of engineering, bridges and aqueducts. The latter were largely the work of Thomas Dadford who also did the original survey. He was a brilliant canal engineer whose route was so good that the canal required only six locks in its 33 miles of length, and five of those were in the $\frac{1}{2}$-mile section of waterway around Llangynydr, 4 miles to the west of Crickhowell.

Except for those going westward from Blorenge to cross the Clydach gorge and climb straight up on to Mynydd Llangattock, all wayfarers will see the canal, as those embarking on the Black Mountains horseshoe cross it at Llanfoist. At Llanfoist the canal user was about halfway between Brecon and Newport. Here the tramway from the forge on Blorenge ended, and the wharf for its barges can still be seen. There were also lime kilns here for the agricultural lime, though landslips have demolished much of the original work. In the village itself the visitor will notice, just opposite the inn for instance, the old track of the Llanfihangel tramway. This was constructed by Hugh Powell, the owner of the Court at Llanfihangel Crucorney a few miles north of Abergavenny, largely for his own benefit. The gauge used was 3'6", larger than normal, and this choice proved far-sighted as the line was eventually taken over by local railway companies who pushed it through to Hereford and Merthyr Tydfil. It was finally axed in the Beeching cuts of the mid-fifties.

Llanfoist was also the birthplace of Capt. Thomas James, variously known as Capt. James of Bristol, Abergavenny or Blaenavon. Despite the additions to his name he was born in the village in the late sixteenth century. In his early twenties he sailed, in 1612, with an expedition to find the North-West Passage. The previous year Henry Hudson had discovered Hudson Bay while attempting to do the same thing, but had later been cast adrift with his 14-year-old son when his crew mutinied. Hudson Bay being inhospitable at the best of times, the pair, adrift without food or adequate clothing, died. It seems that the young James was very impressed by this cautionary tale and when he was forming his own crews in later life he chose only those men who were 'unmarried, approved able and healthy seamen, privately recommended for

Llanfoist village

their ability and faithfulness'. Following his early brush with
northern Canada his life sinks into obscurity but in 1631 the
merchants of Bristol petitioned King Charles I to approve him as
leader of an expedition to find the North-West Passage. He was
duly approved, and sailed in May of that year in the *Henrietta
Maria*. The ship reached Greenland in June and Hudson Bay in
July, but conditions were very bad. James explored the southern
area of Hudson Bay, naming Cape Henrietta Maria and James Bay,
but the ship was entombed in ice in November and he and his crew
spent seven months on the ice awaiting the spring. In May 1632 he
resumed the search for the Passage but in the face of appalling
weather retreated, arriving back in Bristol in October 1632 after a
voyage of almost 18 months. Back in England James wrote a fine
account of the travels and the considerable hardships endured, and
it is widely believed that it was this writing that inspired Coleridge
to write the 'Rimé of the Ancient Mariner'. Capt. James died in
1635.

The suggested route goes over the Black Mountains to reach
Llangattock and then over Mynydd Llangynydr to the Brecon
Beacons. Much of this route, while much described in numerous
walking guides, is an acceptable route only by custom and practice.
Below a route to the Brecon Beacons on rights of way is described
briefly, before the suggested route is described in greater detail.

For those following the canal towpath from Llanfoist to
Llangynydr there is much of interest. The Brecon and Abergavenny
is, arguably, the most beautiful canal in Britain. Since being taken
into the care of the Inland Waterways Board a considerable amount
of work has been carried out on it, and this has made its waters an
asset rather than a sad and stinking reminder of the past. It is
notoriously difficult to outline for visitors the wildlife that they may
see on any stretch of landscape, as invariably that part of the wildlife
is only there if the visitor is not. However, as the canal is such a
delight to the naturalist it is worth noting that quiet and unobtrusive
visitors could see redpolls and siskins as well as the commoner
goldfinches feeding among the alders that are the predominant trees
of the far canal bank. There are willows that house all six of the

Gwryne
Fawr

Five Ways

60   750'

1000'

1250'

1500'

ydd Pen-y-fal

1750' △ Sugar   (596 m
            Loaf   1955')

1500'   1250'

1000'

55

Porth-y-Parc
Farm

A 465
↑ Hereford

750'

500'

A40
khowell/Brecon

250'

Abergavenny

Ysgyryd
Fawr

Castle

50

R. Usk

Llanfoist

commoner British tits, only the crested and bearded tits not being represented. There are tree creepers, nuthatches and woodpeckers, and above the water itself perhaps the blue streak of a kingfisher. Also above the water at the right time of year are dragon and damsel flies, while on it and in it are insects by the score. For the plant enthusiast the water itself holds a typical collection of still-water plants, including lilies, and the stone crevices support a number of our more delicate ferns including the maidenhair and wall-rue spleenworts.

Between Govilon and Gilwern the wayfarer would have crossed from Monmouthshire to Breconshire had not county boundaries been redrawn. Now he has to make 2 more miles westwards before crossing from Mid Glamorgan to Powys.

Near the canal in the section from Llangattock to Talybont can occasionally be found the dwarf elder, known in Welsh as Llysaw Gwaed Gwyr, the herb of the blood of men, from a belief that it could grow only in earth soaked in the blood of Danes killed in battle. Battles with the Danes were fought in the Usk valley during their incursions into Wales.

The canal tow-path is left at Cwm Crawnon (144198) beyond Llangynydr village in favour of the minor road heading south-west towards the Beacons. This is followed until a pathway branches off to the right at (133191). This leads to Bwlch-y-waun (116189) and on to a metalled, though hardly drivable road (110188). This is followed south but at (102177) is left in favour of the pathway going down to the road at (081174). Turn left and follow the road to (049168) where a drivable track leads off right to the Neuadd reservoirs and the suggested route.

From Llanfoist the suggested route continues by roadway to Abergavenny. An alternative is to take the footpath going east along the northern bank of the Usk, branching off left at the obvious break to move directly towards the castle. In view of the history of both town and castle this is an excellent approach, and the river bank here offers a good walk.

Brecon Beacons National Park

Abergavenny

Abergavenny is immediately of interest to those who have but a passing interest in the Welsh language, and who, as a result, believe that the prefix 'Aber . . .' is used only for towns at the mouths of rivers. Indeed so often is the prefix used in this way that it can come as a surprise to learn that the word does not mean 'mouth', but 'confluence'. True the confluence normally referred to is that of river and sea, but here it is river and river, with the Gavenny stream joining the Usk. At this point the Usk is emerging from a fairly tight valley with high peaks on each side, the Brecon Beacons and the Black Mountains. After Abergavenny it flows in more open land on its journey towards Newport and the sea. The town is beautifully situated at the end of the valley. To the south is the mass of Blorenge, and to the west is the Sugar Loaf. To the north is Skirrid, the Anglicised name of the Welsh Ysgyryd. This is an elliptical peak with a deep cleft at one end. The cleft was actually formed by a landslip, but an ancient legend had it that it was split at the time of the Crucifixion. Another version was that the land sank below the weight of Noah's Ark when it came to rest. For either of these two reasons the mountain was held to be sacred and a chapel was built to St. Michael on its summit. This was abandoned long ago and now only a windswept ruin remains on this, the Holy Mountain. Inevitably the Romans, those masters of the art of war, realised the importance of holding the valley-mouth at this junction of streams. They built a fort here naming the site Gobannium from the minor stream. It was probably not lost on the Romans that the stream was itself named from the Welsh (British) name for a blacksmith, because of the iron smelting that was carried out in the area.

The position of the Roman fort was crucial to their defence of Wales, being on the road through the Usk valley from the legion city of Caerleon to Brecon, and on the north-south route from Caerleon to Chester through Wroxeter. For very similar reasons the early Norman marcher lords established a stronghold at the confluence, and a motte and bailey castle was built around 1090. The work was started by the first lord of Abergavenny, Hamelin de Balun, who also founded a Benedictine priory at the site. The original castle was almost certainly wooden, but a stone keep was built in the twelfth century. Following its construction the castle was the scene of several murderous encounters in a story of vengeance between rival Welsh and Norman families. The story can be built from the work of Giraldus, although other sources are required for a complete picture. At the start of the story the lordship of the complete area, Breconshire and Upper Gwent, was to the Earl of Hereford, Milo Fitzwalter. Milo had five sons but each of them died heir-less and so failed to provide a lineage for the title. Because of the lack of a male heir the lordship of the area came to William de Braose, a grandson of Milo through a daughter. At this point Giraldus says that he will 'leave it to others to tell the story of the bloodthirsty outrages which have been committed' and, later, that he has 'thought it better not to relate them in detail, lest they serve to encourage other equally infamous men'. What happened was that de Braose invited Seisyll ap Dyfnwal, who had murdered Milo's third son, his son and some of his followers into the castle 'under a colourable pretext of communication'. Having gathered them together he ordered them to take an oath 'that no traveller by the waie amongst them should beare any bow, or any other unlawful weapon'. Not surprisingly they refused and de Braose condemned them to death, a sentence that was immediately executed by his men. At the same time Seisyll's lands were attacked and another son was murdered. Giraldus's lack of enthusiasm for describing this story may have had more to do with the fact that de Braose was a Norman than any real fear that he might incite murder, for he reports in great detail the attack by Welsh kinsmen of Seisyll seven years later, when the castle was captured and burnt down. There can be little doubt that Giraldus was protecting de Braose, the unspecified events being blamed on anyone rather than him. This is difficult to understand until we remember that Giraldus was Archdeacon of Brecon, and lived at Llanddew only a mile from Brecon castle; and that de Braose held Brecon castle. Giraldus wrote three versions of his journey. In the first he was very hard on

Sugar Loaf

Abergavenny

Hill Road

Avenue Rd

Pen-y-Pound Rd

con

Frogmore St

High St

Town Hall

Cross St

St Mary's Church

Nevill St
St John St

Castle

River Usk

A 465 Heads of Valley Road

A 40 Monmouth

0   ¼ mile
     ½ km

de Braose, but the second shows him in a different light and notes his piety. The third was completed after de Braose's death and Giraldus returns to his critical view. It is not difficult to guess at the reasons for the changes of heart. It seems certain that de Braose was an unpleasant man; confusion surrounds his death but it is likely that following a quarrel with King John he fled, or was exiled, to France. His wife and son were held in Windsor castle probably against his return to face the King, but he failed to return, his family dying of starvation.

Giraldus also recounts with awe an incident during the attack on the castle. When two of the defenders were retreating to the castle over a bridge they were shot at by the Welsh. The arrows missed the men but hit the door to which they were hurrying, splitting it despite its being 'as thick as a man's palm'. He also reports a story by William de Braose which also testified to the power of the bow. In this, a mounted Norman was hit in the leg by an arrow that pierced his leather tunic, his outer iron 'cuish', or leg protector, his leg, his inner cuish, his saddle and finally his horse, killing the horse instantly. As Giraldus says 'it is difficult to see what more you could do, even if you had a ballista'. He also notes that the Welsh bow was made, not of yew, but of elm. It is of little surprise that the English kings later took full advantage of the Welsh bowmen's prowess in their battles in France.

Following the acts of vengeance the castle remained quiet, escaping major damage during the Glyndwr rebellion when the town was burnt, but was largely destroyed by a Parliamentarian army in the Civil War. Now it is a somewhat formless ruin sharing its site with a more modern lodge and the local museum.

In addition to the castle the town was walled, and a walk around that part of it that lay within the walls is very rewarding. From the castle go along Castle Street to the left of which is a row of very fine cottages, gabled and with dormer windows. Beyond the cottages is a barn made of the Old Red Sandstone that gives the mountains of the Brecon Beacons National Park that lie north and west of the town such a distinctive appearance. Turning right after the new Post Office building the walker enters Nevill Street where, to the left near the *King's Arms*, is one of the few remaining sections of the old

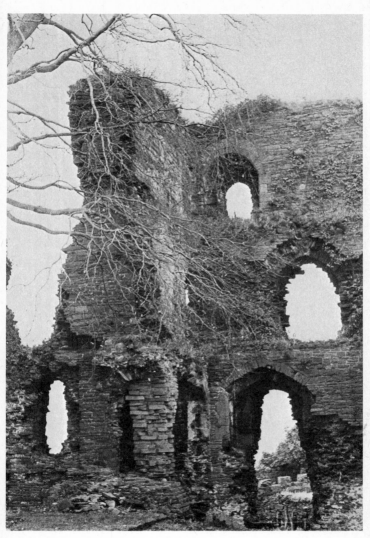

The castle ruins, Abergavenny

wall. Farther down Nevill Street there are several fine Georgian houses, one with a particularly good Adam-style doorway and, opposite these, a house with a row of carved cow's heads below the eaves. This was the *Cow Inn* of the old town. Going right into St. John's Lane and right again into St. John's Street, the visitor reaches the very heart of old Abergavenny. These narrow streets, that would have been cobbled originally, still show the occasional Tudor doorway and are a reminder of the time when the town was a flourishing market town on the border between England and Wales. The streets are named from St. John's church, the original parish church when St. Mary's was the priory church. Now only the tower remains, incorporated into a school named after Henry VIII who by his Acts of Parliament caused the Dissolution of the Monasteries and released the priory church to the town. Turning left at the end of St. John's Street and then left again, the walker enters Flannel Street. Here the name recalls an old industry of the town, the town having been a famous centre for the manufacture of Welsh flannel. It was also famous in the late seventeenth century for the manufacture of periwigs, the full wigs worn by the gentlemen of the day. They were made here from, of all things, goat's hair. Opposite Flannel Street is Market Street with a very fine row of buildings with overhangs supported on wooden pillars above a raised pavement. At the corner of Market Street and Cross Street is the old covered or Butter market which has a very good tower, and next to it is the *King's Head* with an old packhorse archway leading to a courtyard. Farther down Cross Street is the *Angel Inn* which has a Georgian porch built over what was a courtyard arch. With the advent of the stagecoach Abergavenny, because of its position in the Usk valley, became a coaching centre with several inns for overnight stops.

St. Mary's church is a section of the original Benedictine Priory, and a look at the exterior reveals the half-arches and closed doorways that are all that remain, apart from the name Monk Street, of the rest of the monastery. Little of the church dates from the time of the monastery, as it has been rebuilt and restored several times. If the outside is less than exciting the same is not true of the inside for here are some of the finest effigies in Wales. The oldest is

The Jesse tree, St. Mary's Church, Abergavenny

of Eva de Braose who died in 1264 and was a relative of William de
Braose who has already been mentioned. It should be noted that
this attribution has been disputed though the age, some 700 years, is
not in doubt. This, and that of Eva de Canteloupe, are smaller than
life-size, but the fine effigy of George de Canteloupe – the grandson
and son respectively of the two Evas – is true scale. It lies now not
on a tomb, but on a trestle table in the church's central aisle.
Canteloupe died in 1273, this superb carving being over 700 years
old. In its original form it would have been painted, but all traces of
colour are now gone. Pride of place must go to the stone memorial
to Sir William ap Thomas and Gwladys his wife from the
mid-fifteenth century which has excellent effigies lying on a
table-top tomb with some fine and very intricate carving around the
sides. It is a considerable work of art. Another is the Jesse tree
carved from a ten-foot length of solid oak. The tree had a dual

purpose, as a sculpture in its own right – perhaps forming part of a reredos screen – and as a genealogical tree, Jesse being father of David and, therefore, head of the Old Testament dynasty. Now, sadly, only the tree-roots remain, held in the left hand. As long ago as 1587 it was said – 'In this church was a most famous work in manner of a geneologie of kings, called the roote of Jesse, which worke is defaced and pulled down in peeces'. It is still a fine work. Note especially the angel holding a pillow to Jesse's head, and the old man's fatherly beard.

To reach the Black Mountains from Abergavenny it is best to go over Sugar Loaf, as Mynydd Pen-y-fal is more popularly known. With Skirrid it is one of the most popular walking hills in the area, not surprisingly in view of its shape and the panorama from its peak. A sad byproduct of this is the erosion on the pathways to the summit.

To reach Sugar Loaf take Pen-y-pound road out of the town centre and then turn left into Avenue Road which is followed slightly west of north to a car park at (289166). Here bear left through Porth-y-Parc Farm and on to a track that leads to open hillside. Here the wayfarer enters National Trust land, as much of Sugar Loaf is in possession of the Trust. To descend from the summit go north-east to find a stile at (287202) from where a track leads to a minor road at (288204). Go left here and bear right after 300 yards to Five Ways (285211).

From here the route continues to Partrishow. The journey starts with the crossing of Pont-yr-Esgob (284211). Unfortunately the Ordnance Survey have Anglicised the name to Pontysbig on the Leisure map of the Eastern areas of the Beacons National Park. The Welsh 'yr-Esgob' is correct, for this is the Bishop's Bridge. It is named for Archbishop Baldwin who was the travelling companion of Giraldus – or, more correctly, the reverse is true. Giraldus himself makes no mention of the bridge, or of nearby Partrishow. He notes that from Llanddew 'we made our way along the rugged pass of Coed Grwyne . . . by a narrow trackway overgrown with trees'. Giraldus may have been apprehensive of the journey as he notes that it was near here that Richard de Clare 'a nobleman of

Pont-yr-Esgob, the Bishop's Bridge

high birth . . . who . . . held Cardiganshire' was ambushed by
Welshmen under one 'Iorwerth, the brother of Morgan of Caerleon'
and killed. That was in 1136 but things had changed for the better
by 1188 as a local legend has it that it was at this point that the
locals placed stepping-stones across the ford so that the travellers
could cross without wetting their feet. These stones were the first
'bridge' but the honour of usage by Baldwin earned the spot its
name.

   After the bridge go uphill and right at the fork. Here take the
track right to the ruined Ty Mawr Farm (282215). Go right then left
along the far side of the next hedge to the road. Go right and follow
the road to Partrishow church. This corner of the National Park is
poorly served by roads and maintains a quiet, almost timeless,
quality. As the road bends right to go uphill to the church a flat slab
marked with a Maltese cross lies to the right. The slab points to the

Holy Well of St. Ishow. Ishow was a mystic, a hermit who lived in a cell near here having shunned the world of men. To any traveller he would show kindness and hospitality and attempt to win them over to a Christian way of life. One day a traveller murdered him for his pitifully few possessions. There the story might have ended had it not been for a visit to the spot of a high-born lady who had contracted leprosy during a trip to Europe. She drank from the well and was cured, and was so delighted that she filled the niches with gold, which was used to build the church. The well is still there. The church itself was built close to the site of the miracle, and is, as a result, very remote. Happily its very remoteness has meant that time, and restorers, have passed it by, and, though altered and now largely medieval, it is very much today as it must have been when it was first built. Inside it is a treasure house. The font is the oldest item, dating from the eleventh century. It is the rood screen that draws the visitor, however. Such screens were common in the medieval churches, they carried the rood or cross and formed the frontage of a gallery that held the choir and, in earliest times, musicians. The gallery also allowed access to the rood itself so that it could be decorated with flowers during the various festivals throughout the year. This practice, as with murals and other 'idolatrous' ideas, appalled the Puritans and that, together with later, chiefly Victorian, vicars who wanted more space caused the majority of screens and galleries to be removed. The almost complete screen here is therefore a major survival. It is also a masterpiece. The design is a repetition of a basic dragon and vine theme, probably to represent evil, the dragon consuming good, the vine, but never finally triumphing because of the all-powerful good, represented by the cross that would have been fixed above. The work is said, with little or no supporting evidence, to be the work of an Italian woodcarver who was employed at nearby Llanthony Abbey. Perhaps the legend grew from the idea that no Welshman would know how a vine looked.

It is hard to believe when considering this work of art that one of the reasons why the screen was extended to the floor – apart from the support this offered – and why altar rails were included in church designs after the discontinuation of screening was to prevent dogs, who invariably accompanied their owners into the church, from fouling the altar!

A further medieval feature that would have incensed the Puritans is the fine mural on the west wall. This is a 'doom' figure, Father Time as a skeleton to represent death. Here it was painted near the exit so that the worshippers could see it as they departed and so recognise their eventual fate and their only true salvation.

The church also retains a stone altar, in fact not one but two, each a memorial of the pre-Elizabethan days when the altar table was made from the tombstone of a martyr. At the time of Elizabeth it was ordered that such altars were to be destroyed and replaced by wooden tables, so the two here, at the base of the rood screen, are a remarkable find. Each has its five consecration crosses – one for each of the wounds of Christ. More remarkable still is the fact that the church actually has a third stone altar. This is situated in the odd little cell attached to the west wall. The room has a window allowing a view of the service, and may have been used by a particularly devout worshipper. Oddly the altar in the cell has six crosses instead of the usual five.

The visitor will also notice the excellent cradle-roof of oak, and the stone benches that line the walls of the church. The latter were used by the old and sick in the days when there were no seats or pews in churches and are the origin of the expression – 'the old go to the wall'. Altogether this is a most delightful place.

To continue go eastward through the churchyard, and down the path to Ty'n-y-llwyn Farm (281223). From this track, looking back, the church is a fine sight, nestling in its shrub cover across the grass. Those who approach from this eastern side are offered a more spectacular first show, as only after they have visited the church are they likely to realise that it can be reached by road rather than by walking or riding across fields. After the farm building a gate on the left gives access to an indistinct path, becoming less so, that leads directly to the road at (284226). Alternatively the farm lane is followed down to the road at (284223). Go left to a road down to the river and the chapel on its far side (284227). From the chapel take a footpath north-east to a lane at (287229). The lane is followed to (289228) where the walker goes right on a track to Carreg y Dial.

Partrishow Church

Carreg y Dial or, as the Ordnance Survey has it, Dialgarreg, is the
Stone of Revenge, and was erected, so it is said, to commemorate
the ambush and murder of Richard de Clare, an event mentioned
earlier as having been recorded by Giraldus. De Clare had earlier
made several attacks on the Welsh in order to secure further land,
and was on his way to Cardigan. The local lord, Brian de
Wallingford, accompanied de Clare as far as here to guide him
through the 'pass', presumably the valley of the Grwyne Fawr.
Despite de Wallingford's wishes and 'indeed, against his express
advice' de Clare dismissed him and continued with only a small
group of men. This would have been foolish enough, but de Clare
sent ahead of the party a singer and fiddler to announce his coming.
The party was ambushed and cut down, their baggage being stolen.
After presenting the facts Giraldus launches into an attack on those
who are 'so presumptuous'. He reminds us that 'to rush on

The doom figure, a mural in Partrishow Church

regardless is simply false bravado. It is at once rash and inconsiderate to take no heed at all of the advice given by those who are trying to help us.' This is not only a lesson from the Archdeacon, but Giraldus talking as a good Norman for shortly after de Clare's murder the Welsh defeated the English at the Battle of Crug Mawr near Cardigan largely, or so says Giraldus, due to an absence of the leader (de Clare) on the English side. It is not clear who erected the stone, but it is certain that the present stone is not the first, an earlier one having been larger. Nor is it clear precisely where the ambush took place. Giraldus calls the wood simply Grwyne wood which would imply that it was in the valley at the foot of the ridge. Possibly the truth is that the association of stone and story is legendary, and that, as has been suggested, the stone is in fact an ancient sundial-cum-marker used by the Welsh cattle drovers en route for the Vale of Ewyas and Gospel Pass. The name would then have been 'deial' (for dial) instead of 'dial' (for revenge) though the two pronounciations are the same allowing considerable scope for interchange. Beyond Carreg y Dial are the Black Mountains.

The Black Mountains are the most easterly of the blocks of Old Red Sandstone peaks that make up the Brecon Beacons National Park. As with the other blocks the most characteristic feature is the escarpment, here facing north-west, although there are no corrie lakes, and the area is split by striking valleys. The valleys run north-south, draining down to the Usk valley, and so deep do they cut into the sandstone mass that they have created a series of parallel ridges. To the east is the Hatterrall Hill to Hay Bluff ridge, taken by the Offa's Dyke long-distance footpath, separated by the magnificent Vale of Ewyas from the main mass of the Mountains. In this main mass there is a continuous ridge-top to the escarpment, the valleys of the Grwyne Fawr and Grwyne Fechan having failed to cut back to the escarpment itself. The geography is, therefore, of a trident, the three prongs ending at Bal Mawr, Crug Mawr and Pen Cerrig-calch. To the west there is a small outlying group of peaks lying between the Rhian-goll stream and Llangorse lake. The ridges created by these valleys are wide and whale-backed, the valleys themselves being wooded and having a secluded peaceful air.

Though the Mountains comprise wide grassy ridges there are

some peat deposits which, particularly at the summit of Waun Fach, create difficult walking where the peat is deeply trenched and wet. Despite this the ridges make walking relatively safe, but the traveller should beware, for in addition to all the dangers that may befall the unwary in bad weather there is also the 'old lady' of the Black Mountains, a spectral figure who may appear to lead him astray.

As well as peat there are heather beds, particularly to the north, which attract large numbers of butterflies. Because of the heavily-grazed grassland that predominates, the upland birdlife is chiefly limited to members of the crow and lark families. In the valleys the situation is much improved, the Grwyne Fawr stream holding a number of dippers and grey wagtails, while the mixed woodland at stream level attracts a great variety of small birds.

From Carreg y Dial the route continues straightforwardly to Garn-wen, and on to Bal Mawr, and from there a reasonable path leads on along the ridge towards the escarpment. To the east from here, and well worth the walk to the ridge edge, is the Vale of Ewyas. This has long been the favourite of the valleys that bury themselves deep into the Black Mountains, one reason being that at its head there is a pass between the peaks of Twmpa and Hay Bluff.

The Black Mountains escarpment from Twmpa

This is Gospel Pass, named from a straightforward translation of the Welsh Bwlch yr Efengyl. The Welsh name derives from a legend that a daughter of Caratacus, the Silurian leader at the time of the Roman invasion, invited St. Peter and St. Paul to come and preach the gospel to her tribesmen. They came, and in their journey to, or from, the Usk valley they used this pass.

Another reason that the Ewyas vale is famous is because of its beauty. The high ridge from Hatterrall Hill to Hay Bluff to the east and the present ridge to the west, ensure the valley a wonderful quiet and calm, as well as giving a wonderful backdrop to any view in the valley itself. The view to the east of Bal Mawr is dominated by the ruins of Llanthony Priory. The ruins are impressive, but do not have the completeness or the dignity of, say, nearby Tintern Abbey. But they are wonderfully positioned and it is easy to see why William de Lacy, the founder, chose to stay when he came here towards the end of the twelfth century weary, or so it is said, of his life of vice and sin. De Lacy is said to have worn his armour as a hair shirt until it rusted and fell off with age. There was a church here even at that time, but de Lacy wanted a more profoundly spiritual environment – in keeping with the serenity of the site perhaps – and founded an Augustinian priory. Giraldus recounts a story dealing with the building of the priory in the first person suggesting that he may have been a party to it. The priory, he says, was built with blocks of 'marble' called freestones that were to be found lying on the mountain-side and 'they have this remarkable property, that you can search until you are quite exhausted and collect all these freestones, until none is left and no more could possibly be found, and then, three or four days later, you can look again and there they all are, just as numerous as before, easy to find if you look, and there for you to take.'

Those heading for the Youth Hostel at Capel-y-ffin can ascend the Vale of Ewyas without regaining the ridge. The 'main' road need not be taken as a minor road also ascends the valley on the eastern side of the river. For those who have not visited Llanthony, beyond Bal Mawr the route is easy, towards the escarpment. It is best at the northern end to avoid the temptation to contour around the head of the Grwyne Fawr cwm, the apparent distance that can

be saved being more than made up for in the time lost on
unremitting vegetation. The tracks, badly eroded by pony-trekkers
who appear from time to time in 7th cavalry numbers, do at least
offer reasonable walking. The wayfarer is now heading for Waun
Fach, the 'little moor' that is the highest point of the range. It is not
the 'high point' as well, the summit being a large white circular slab,
a trig. point base, usually daubed in red or blue, presumably
marking trek paths. In wet weather it can actually be difficult to
reach, the slab lying in the middle of a small peat bog, but it is of
little consequence as the ground for many yards in all directions is at
the same altitude. South-east from Waun Fach is the only real peak
on the range, Pen y Gader Fawr, a fine summit with a good cairn.
Those who wish to include the peak can continue along the path
beside the forestry plantations to Crug Mawr from where a track
leads down to Llanbedr village. From there a minor road leads
down to Crickhowell. The better route is to follow the ridge that
leads south from Pen Trumau, a top to the west of Waun Fach. The
ridge is followed to Pen Allt-mawr, a steep climb preceding the trig.
point. This is, perhaps, the best ridge walk in south Wales, and rivals
many an expedition in the north. The walking is never strenuous,
though sometimes a little difficult, and the views are superb.
Because the ridge is a very wide whale-back the eye is drawn away
from the immediate valleys, a little hidden below the curve of the
land, to the distant hills, plains and valleys. The Black Mountains
horseshoe walk – starting from Llanbedr and going out via Crug
Mawr and Pen y Gader Fawr to Waun Fach, and returning along
this ridge – is understandably popular, and deserves inclusion in any
Welsh walker's itinerary.

The route from Pen Allt-mawr continues along the ridge to Pen
Cerrig-calch, an interesting peak as its summit is the final surviving
section of the limestone sheet that once overlaid the sandstone, and
still does on the Llangattock escarpment. The name is descriptive of
this limestone cap, evidence of the understanding the early Welsh
farmers had of their land before the science of geology revealed the
existence and significance of this outlying sheet. From the limestone
cap the wayfarer makes his way down east of south to the obvious

Llanthony Priory in the Vale of Ewyas

feature of Table Mountain which, as will be mentioned later, is defined by the remains of a hill-fort after which the town of Crickhowell is named. From the southern edge of the flat-topped peak descend south-west to a house (Dol-y-gaer) from where a track, waymarked beyond the house, leads south to a farm (Wern), and on to a minor road which is followed into Crickhowell.

Crickhowell

Crickhowell lies in the shadow of Table Mountain, not as famous as its South African counterpart perhaps but just as well named. The Welsh name is Crug Hywel, Hywel's hill, said to derive from Hywel Dda (Hywel the Good) the famous law-giver whose statue is amongst those of the Welsh heroes in Cardiff's Civic Centre. Hywel was an early tenth-century leader and it is possible that the hill-fort that stands on top of the hill was occupied around that time. Its general layout is typically Iron Age, which would mean that it pre-dated Hywel by a thousand years. The length and steepness of the approach on all but the northern side must have made the fort a formidable site, and its position in the lower part of the Usk valley, guarding the valley itself, was also crucial. The Normans with their improved castle building techniques could afford to place a lord at Tretower, the more strategically correct site, but they did not ignore Crickhowell. The ruins we now see in the town are those of the castle built by a later lord with the unlikely name of Sir Grimbaud Pauncefoot in the latter part of the thirteenth century. It was Sir Grimbaud's wife, Lady Sybil, who was co-founder of the church and it is believed that the effigies within it, at the side of the altar, are of the Knight and his Lady. Even though Pauncefoot was more English than Norman it is still interesting that the dedication of the church is to St. Edmund, the adopted son of Offa the Saxon King who built the dyke between England and Wales. In its complete form the castle had a shell keep, as at Tretower, around a motte from the original construction, and a wall with towers from later phases of work. Additions were being made right up to the time of the Glyndwr revolt but following that, when it was almost completely destroyed, there was neither renovation nor addition. Thereafter the site became a dependable and easily accessible quarry, and as lately as the 1900's there was a major collapse. Now all that remain are the ivy-clad ruins of the gatehouse tower and portcullis gate. The old motte is known affectionately as The Tump, while the whole has acquired the name Alisby's Castle from a later owner.

Using the castle as a starting point the traveller will be well rewarded for the effort of taking a short walk around the town. In Castle Street is the Presbyterian Danycastell chapel. Now go across the top of Bridge Street and through Lamb Lane to New Road. To the left here is a building that was once a flannel mill, Crickhowell having been once an important manufacturing centre, as was nearby Abergavenny. To the right is the church of St. Edmund. Little of the building dates from the first mentioned period, and there was considerable restoration in the nineteenth century. Much that is fine remains, however, particularly the reredos and some of the earlier

Crickhowell, the Usk Bridge and Table Mountain

windows. Neither has the restoration been without its successes.
This is especially true of the spire that was rebuilt in 1861 to the
design of the architect of some of the restorations of Westminster
Abbey, J. Pearson. Unhappily the financing of the spire was not as
harmonious as the design and caused considerable local argument
and, eventually, reached the courts. Continuing up New Road the
traveller arrives at the main A40. To the left here is Porth Mawr,
the Big Gate. Indeed it is a large castellated gatehouse, finely set in
a length of solid stone wall. Behind this imposing structure there is –
nothing! At one time there was of course, but Cwrt-y-Carw, Stag
Court, built in Tudor times for the Hubert family, has long since
gone. West from here is Gwernvale, once a manor house in which
was born, in 1790, Sir George Everest whose name is now world
famous, having been given to a mountain when it was discovered to
be the highest in the world while Sir George was Surveyor General
of India.

Turning right at Porth Mawr the traveller heads back towards the centre of the town passing the *Bear Hotel*, another of the coaching inns that lined the Usk valley route down to the Severn. It is thought that the imposing Georgian front is superimposed on an older building. Our route now goes through the Square and down High Street to the steep Bridge Street. This is from the eighteenth century and is complete with cobbled pavements and bow-fronted shops. At the bottom is the *Bridge End Inn* whose wrap-around look derives from the foundations of the Octagonal Toll House on which it stands. The bridge itself is one of the high points of a trip around the town. The present one dates, in the main, from 1706 when it was stone-built at a cost of £400. When it was first widened and then modified to accept the New Road in the early nineteenth century, the bridge acquired an imbalance. If the traveller checks he will discover that there are 13 arches on one side, but only 12 on the other.

Beyond the bridge is Llangattock, a little south of which the Brecon and Abergavenny canal is reached again. Here too, as at Llanfoist, there are lime-kilns. Initially, as a study of the Llangattock escarpment by wayfarers who visit it will show, the kilns were at the quarries. With the advent of improved transport however it was decided to move stone to the canal by tramway, to create the kilns at the wharves and ship out the prepared lime. The kilns at Llangattock were served by a tramway that came down inclines from the escarpment quarries. Lime was also carried to the ironworks at Beaufort. The village itself is a quiet place ambling gently back up the hill towards the escarpment that takes its name. The name derives from St. Catwg, another of the many early Celtic Christians, and the church to him is interesting in still possessing, inside, the old village stocks and whipping-post.

From Llangattock the suggested route follows the minor road south, or the track that exits south from it at the left-hand bend (206169), to the Llangattock escarpment. On Mynydd Llangattock and Mynydd Llangynydr the rights of way run north-south, not east-west, but there is considerable literature on east-west crossings, and many walkers tramp the moorland at weekends. The right-of-way route from here follows the canal tow-path to Llangynydr as detailed above.

⑨⓪

Brecon

Dol-y-gaer 1250'

1000'

750' The Wern 500'

Crickhowell

250'

Llangynidr

R. Usk

250'

Llangattock

Castle

A40 Abergavenny

A4077 Gilwern

Monmouthshire & Brecon Canal Llanfoist

500'

Clydach Gorge

⑨⑤

Agen Allwedd Cave 750' 1000'

Eglwys Faen Cave 1250'

1500'

Pwll Gwyrhoc

Mynydd Llangattock

Llangynidr

(541m △1775')

⑩⓪

B4560 Brynmawr

1500' 1750' 1750'

Chartist's Cave

Llyn y Garn-fawr

Mynydd Llangynidr

1500'

500'

⑩⑤

1750'

Quarries

The escarpment itself is interesting far beyond the industrial archaeology of the kilns and tramway. Here the limestone 'bursts out along the whole range of mountains' as it was said in 1805, and that is true for the escarpment reveals the limestone from under the millstone cover. Above the cliffs there are a large number of instances where the caves in the underlying limestone have collapsed causing stoke holes. In addition the impervious millstone has allowed some hollows to fill with water causing ponds to appear where the wayfarer does not expect ponds to be. One such is Pwll Gwyrhoc, the witches' pond. That is just how it feels, for on this stretch of moorland the visitor is usually alone, and it is surprising to come upon this large, dark stretch of water, its edges half-hidden among the bilberries. In the right conditions of wind and mist it would come as no surprise to hear the cackling laughter of Macbeth's witches.

The major part of the escarpment, the western end, forms the Craig y Ciliau nature reserve, nominated for its plant life. Here there are many fine limestone plants that are found in few other, if any, places in Britain. The chief interest, however, lies in the six very rare species of the genus sorbus that grow there. These shrubs or small trees, rowans and whitebeams, grow, in general, high on the cliff faces, but great care should be taken by the wayfarer to avoid damaging any plant life in the area. It hardly needs stressing that the picking of flowers is out of the question.

At the foot of the limestone cliffs there are several caves the entrances to which have been quarried. The largest entrances are of 'Eglwys Faen', the stone church, which occurs as the tramroad swings sharply right. The numerous entrances all lead to the same cave system, but the largest entrance, up and right facing the cliff, leads directly into the huge chamber that gives the cave its name. The wayfarer can comfortably penetrate the chamber for some distance in daylight alone, but should take great care as the floor is littered with ankle-turning stones.

Farther along the pathway is the entrance to Agen Allwedd, the keyhole cave, gated so that the inexperienced cannot enter. The reason for this is straightforward for beyond the gate are 29 kilometres of passageway. At one time this was the longest cave

Mynydd Llangattock escarpment

system known in Britain, and it could be once again if the anticipated link with the cave Ogof Craig-y-ffynnon on the far side of the hill is ever made.

From the caves the route strikes westward, crossing the B4560 and heading for Chartists' cave at (127152). The moorland is barren here and great care should be taken. The walking is not particularly easy, the whole being a good introduction to the land of Elenydd farther north. The cave has a single large chamber with two smaller chambers leading off, and was the hiding place for leaders of the Chartist movement in South Wales before the march on Newport. Chartism is a movement whose name is well-known but whose true significance is most often unknown or misunderstood. The cave is a good shelter and resting spot to contemplate the social conditions of the first third of the nineteenth century.

Chartism

The strikes and upsurge of unionism that we have seen occurred in the mining and ironmaking communities were directed primarily against the poverty of their working lives, but contained an element of resentment against the whole of the existing social order. The Poor Law of 1834 with its workhouses and, more importantly, the idea that the poor were responsible for, and should be made to suffer for, their poverty caused unrest. Few of those in power had any sympathy with Cobbett's idea that a pauper was only a very poor man, and the unsympathetic nature of their law caused great resentment in those affected. After the years of bad working and living conditions, repression by force if necessary and injustice, resentment boiled over and became a movement that touched every part of Britain. The movement was known as Chartism because its followers supported the People's Charter published in 1838, a six-point plan for Parliamentary reform demanding universal male suffrage; equal electoral districts; secret ballots; abolition of property qualifications for Members of Parliament; payment of Members; and annual Parliaments. Now, with five points of the charter accepted and the sixth, annual Parliaments, not felt to be a practical proposition by any credible organisation, it is difficult to understand the threat to the established order that the charter represented.

In South Wales the Chartists' leader was John Frost, a man of 55 in the fateful year of 1839. By 1839 the Chartists' leaders became convinced that attempts to achieve some reforms, or even discussion of their grievances, were doomed to failure and some began to argue in favour of direct action. A general strike was called for August, but this never occurred. Eventually in November Frost, convinced that the men of the Midlands and North were ready to rise up and seize power, decided to give the lead by organising the men of South Wales to capture Newport. In secret he advised local leaders and soon there were men hiding in wait in this cave, and others in the caves of the Llangattock escarpment making weapons. On 3 November all was ready and the men started to make their way into the Ebbw valley and down it to Risca. The weather was appalling and far fewer men than expected arrived at the town.

They were also badly armed, many having only pitchforks with them. Frost had hoped to be able to command as many as 50,000 men but he had many fewer than that. The Chartists themselves later claimed it was as few as 400, though the mayor of Newport claimed 20,000. Neither figure is likely to be correct with each side exaggerating to its own ends, and it is likely that Frost had 5,000 men when he marched to Newport on 4 November. As happened previously the mayor assumed command of the small band of soldiers, about 30 in number, in the town and stationed them at the *Westgate Hotel*. There was an exchange of words between the two sides, but communication in the real sense was beyond hope. A shot was fired, each side claiming after that the other fired first, and the soldiers immediately fired a volley into the crowd, continuing to fire haphazardly for about ten minutes more. The Chartists, not surprisingly in view of their condition, turned and fled leaving 22 men behind dead or dying. Frost was captured soon after and was tried with seven other local leaders for treason. They were found guilty and sentenced to death by hanging, that to be followed by decapitation and quartering. In order to avoid a sympathetic backlash the sentences were commuted, and Frost was transported to Van Diemen's Land. Fifteen years later Frost was pardoned and returned to Britain white-haired but still a strong-willed man. He died in 1877 at the great age of 93.

Following the Newport rebellion Chartism declined in Wales, not surprisingly as a great number of people were appalled by the uprising, regardless of its justification. From 1839 onwards the workers followed the less dangerous pathway of local strikes.

Our route continues across trackless and difficult ground towards the Beacons. There is little shelter here and few landmarks, even the cave being easy to miss if conditions are less than perfect. Head west, but go south of the quarries of Pistyll Crawnon. A right of way goes north of these on the southern edge of the forest, but this involves crossing fences where the right of way ends. The southern route keeps to open moorland traversing above the quarries to (085148). From here go north-west, heading for a landmark, the summit of Pant y Creigiau at (056162). This latter section is marshy, but offers an expanding view of the Brecon Beacons. From

the summit descent is made to the minor road at (050167) where
the route from the canal tow-path is rejoined. Continue easily to the
Neuadd reservoirs and the Brecon Beacons.

Brecon Beacons
The mass of the Brecon Beacons is the most distinctive in the
National Park, the truncated summits of Corn Du and Pen y Fan
being easily distinguished from almost any direction. The scenery
here is similar to Waun Fach on the Black Mountains in the eastern
section of the mass where it forms a plateau at around 2,400 feet
which extends over about one square mile around Gwaen
Cerrig-llwydion and Waen-rydd. Here the peat outcrops are so deep
that the walker can trek between them, an almost lunar landscape.
This is an isolated example of true similarity, however, for the
Beacons are characterised more by the glacially-hollowed U-valleys
to the north than by river valleys. Particularly fine is Cwm Oergwm,
to the east of Pen y Fan itself. The escarpment face, particularly on
the higher peaks, also appears more precipitous and this, together
with the corrie lake, Llyn-cwm-llwch, gives the mass a more
mountainous, less pastoral quality.
    The route follows the Roman road in towards the pass to the east
of Cribyn, before moving off left (west) to follow the (too) well
marked path up to Pen y Fan summit. This is the highest peak in
South Wales, and fails by only 93 feet to be the fifteenth 3,000-foot
peak in Wales. There is no denying the very real attraction of
Pen y Fan, the steep northern face more than making up, from a
'mountain' point of view, for the curious flat top, but the popularity
of it can detract from its attractiveness if it is swarming with
weekend walkers. This is a sad but necessary by-product of freedom
of access.
    From the summit of Pen y Fan and nearby Corn Du the view is
extensive, over mid-Wales to Plynlimon and over South Wales.
From Corn Du there are several ways off to the west. Those going
to the Youth Hostel can go north-west down the ridge that passes
the Tommy Jones memorial obelisk at (000217). Tommy was the
five-year-old son of a Welsh miner who came to the Beacons in

1900 to visit his grandfather. They were walking from Brecon when they met the boy's grandfather and cousin. Tommy and his cousin ran on to the grandfather's farm, but after a short distance the boy ran back to rejoin his father. He never arrived and an extensive search failed to locate him. It was almost a month later that his body was found at this spot a long way from where he was last seen. At the time the disappearance was headline news but doubtless it would now be forgotten if the obelisk had not been erected. It is a timely reminder of the risk inherent in a walk over the Welsh mountains by anyone, of any age.

Those not going down to the Youth Hostel can descend south-west to reach the A470 to the south of the *Storey Arms*.

Immediately to the west of the A470 now is Fforest Fawr, the Great Forest of the Lords of Brecon. As usual the word forest here causes confusion at a time when forest for most of us means regimented rows of Forestry Commission conifers. In Saxon and medieval times a forest was simply a hunting ground. Now the name is applied to the moorland between the A470 and A4067, containing the distinctive peaks of Fan Fawr to the east and Fan Gihirych to the west. On Ordnance Survey maps the name is applied also to the land in Mynydd Ddu, as far as Fan Hir, which conforms to the official Norman forest. From the A470 near the *Storey Arms* the ascent of Fan Fawr is straightforward and is accomplished by numbers of walkers each weekend. It is equally straightforward to continue westward around the northern end of the Ystradfellte reservoir over Fan Llia to the minor road around (924194). From there the ascent of Fan Gihirych is accomplished by going north of Fan Nedd. None of this route is on public footpaths, and although the Cnewr estate which owns the western, Fan Gihirych, section is tolerant of walkers in principle, they are unhappy about any trespass in the lambing season, say 1 January until Easter. It is strongly suggested therefore that this area of Fforest Fawr be avoided. Unlike other upland areas of Wales there are few guide books that suggest the traverse as an acceptable route, so custom and practice cannot be claimed. Clearly it would be better to avoid the area and go instead for the waterfall country to the south which, in any case, offers a change from the sandstone already

Corn Du, Pen y Fan and Cribyn on the Brecon Beacons

traversed and still to come.

To the south of Fforest Fawr the scenery changes remarkably, the escarpments and grassed ridges of the Old Red Sandstone giving way to deeply cut and wooded valleys of limestone country with waterfalls and caves. The valleys of the Hepste and Mellte rivers are little more than 10 miles from Merthyr Tydfil and yet the contrast between these delightful valleys and those of the South Wales Coalfield could not be greater. Unfortunately there is no other way to enter the valleys than to follow the A4059, although as the road is unfenced the wayfarer can cross the moorland on either side of the road. The Hepste river, which is soon reached, is an interesting river, for long periods running underground so that its stream bed is dry. A short cut, by minor road direct to Ystradfellte, is reached at (944105) a mile from Penderyn village from which the Hepste valley can be reached. Leave the village from its northern edge

(944089) past houses and on to a signposted track, going to the right, not left, to Tor Foel Farm. Take the track downhill into the valley and follow the valley downstream.

The first fall reached, Sgwd yr Eira, the spout of snow, is also the most famous, because the visitor can walk behind the curtain of water which is pushed out 3 feet by the overhang of rock at the fall head. This is, in fact, the only crossing point of the Hepste in the valley and was used at one time by farmers moving sheep from one side of the valley to the other. Great care must be taken as the rocks behind the water are very slippery. Though Sgwd yr Eira is the most famous and interesting of the falls it is only the beginning. The route now strikes off north-west to the Mellte valley. There is a path, but it can be overgrown and difficult to follow. However with care, and never leaving the river too far away, the northern bank of the Hepste is left and the eastern bank of the Mellte joined. The first Mellte fall is Sgwd y Pannwr, the smallest, though still picturesque. Next is Sgwd Isaf Clun-gwyn which has a smoothly curved top giving it the look of a major fall. Last is Sgwd Clun-gwyn, but even that is not the end for farther on is the resurgence of the Mellte river. From here to Porth yr Ogof the river is underground for about 400 yards although at a couple of points on the pathway there are holes through which the river can be glimpsed. Porth-yr-Ogof is reached by a short walk from the minor road that is reached after the potholes. This is one of the most spectacular cave entrances in Britain, the Mellte river being engulfed in the letter-box slot hole in the rock. When in torrent the river fills the slot, but usually the entrance can be explored without need for a torch for about 40 yards, to the Pool of the White Horse. The pool is named from the calcite streaks on the wall that resemble a horse's head. The white horse forms part of a legend, a Welsh princess having ridden into the cave to escape a pursuer and having drowned. Sadly the drowning has been repeated several times in reality as the waters can make a full investigation of the cave a dangerous undertaking. Some of those who have died have been experienced cavers. From Porth-yr-Ogof the Youth Hostel is reached straightforwardly by reversing to the minor road and going west. The village of Ystradfellte is reached by turning right, instead of left for the

Sgwd Clun-gwyn

Hostel, at the T-junction. The village is a quiet place with a shop and inn, and a largely restored church among some very ancient yew trees. Michael Faraday, the famous nineteenth-century scientist, stayed here, coming, as we have, to see the waterfalls. The village can also boast a Castell Coch, the ruin on private land of a thirteenth-century sandstone castle.

Leave Ystradfellte along the metalled lane to the side of the *New Inn*. At the turn-off to Tyle Farm (926134) carry straight on. At (924138) there is a footpath leading off across the moor slightly north of west to the minor road at (913142). Turn right and go to Blaen-nedd-isaf Farm. Here a footpath is signposted westward over a footbridge south of the farm. Just beyond the farm the footpath crosses Sarn Helen, a Roman road named either after a Welsh princess whom we shall encounter again at Croesor in Snowdonia, as we near the end of our journey, or after Lleon the Mighty.

The Mellte river above the waterfalls

Beyond the Roman road there is excellent walking on open moor to the quarries at Penwyllt (856156).

Under the quarries is Ogof ffynnon ddu, the cave of the black spring. There are three entrances to the cave, widely separated, the separation giving some idea of what lies below the surface. For here is a cave system which at 38 kilometres is the second longest in Britain, only the 45 kilometres Lancaster Hole/Easegill/Link Pot system below Gregareth in Yorkshire being longer, and, at 300 metres, it is the deepest in Britain. Not only is it enormous, but it is also extremely complex having what is widely believed to be the most dazzling three-dimensional array of passages of any cave in Britain. Not surprisingly it is kept locked, the key being given only to established caving clubs.

The wayfarer may follow the old, now trackless, railway line to the head of the minor road at Penwyllt (854158), or he may go directly for the road, which is unfenced on its south-eastern side around the quarry at (851155). There is a very slight confusion here in that a footpath is signed at (854158), where one is not marked by the Ordnance Survey, while only one of the two near (851155) is marked. The way forward is clear however. From (851155) the walker either takes a south-westerly route down towards the river Tawe and then swings northward to reach and cross the river and hence reach the A4067 at (842160), or he goes almost due north to Pwll-Coediog (849164) and follows the lane to the A4067. The decision depends upon whether he wishes to visit the Dan-yr-Ogof show caves.

A little down the valley from Dan-yr-Ogof is Craig-y-nos Castle started in 1842 but completed by the famous opera singer Dame Adelina Patti during her residence from 1879 until her death in 1919. It is now a hospital.

Leaving the caves the wayfarer goes north along the A4067 to reach the second route at (847167). Continue north again to the *Tafarn-y-Garreg* inn. Opposite it a footpath is signed to a new bridge over the Tawe, and Mynydd Ddu beyond. The name Mynydd Ddu is Welsh for Black Mountain, and that latter English form has been used extensively, the lack of the plural 's' being the only way of distinguishing this most westerly sandstone mass from

the eastern Black Mountains. Another English form is Camarthen Fan, a pseudo-Welsh name, fan meaning 'top' or high point. The Welsh name is preferred here, both to avoid confusion, and to lend a little mystery, for this is the most mysterious and desolate of the Beacons' masses. Its northern edge has the, by now, usual escarpment and here it is both very steep and very long and continues along the eastern edge of the mass, so that it broods over the lakes Llyn y fan fawr and Llyn y fan fach. Behind the scarp, however, lies a shallow dip slope that extends a considerable distance westward and southward to form an upland plateau, in places boggy, that has a wild and desolate air. This almost featureless plateau is land for the connoisseur. To add to the mystery there are a number of menhirs in the area and, in addition, at Cerrig Duon (851206) one of the few Welsh stone alignments. The site consists of a circle of small stones, some 2 feet high, about 60 feet in diameter with an avenue of stones leading away to the north-east and a single large stone, 6 feet high, 10 yards to the north. The stones have been vandalised by name-scratchers, but the site has a distinct atmosphere, assisted doubtless by its wind-swept nature and the backdrop of the long ridge of Fan Hir.

   Cerrig Duon is worth visiting, though this sadly means a detour. After the site, however, things improve significantly, the wayfarer following the Nant y Llyn back to Llyn y fan fawr, ascending the slope to Bannau Brycheniog and continuing around the escarpment until above Llyn y fan fach. Here though steep the scarp slope is easily descended to the lakeside.·

   The last route description does indeed offer the best continuation, those not visiting Cerrig Duon continuing from the Tawe bridge up Fan Hir to the trig.-point summit. This is a much travelled and published route though the only true right of way crosses the southern moorland heading north-west and then north to Llanddeusant. This route should be treated with great caution. The area crossed is difficult and desolate, and is also of great scientific interest and, therefore, sensitive to invasion. On balance it is preferable to continue to Llyn y fan fach via the escarpment. The high point is Bannau Brycheiniog, the horns of Brecon, although this name is more appropriately applied to the escarpment

Looking south over Cerrig Duon stone circle, Mynydd Ddu

immediately north of the summit, which does indeed have a
hornlike appearance. Bannau Sir Gaer, the horns of Camarthen –
before the redefining of Welsh counties the summit plateau was the
county boundary – are less horn-like but an arc of steep and high
escarpment does brood over one of the finest of lakeland sites.

Llyn y fan fach
Llyn y fan fach is the site of one of the most fascinating of all Welsh
folk legends, the story of the lady of the lake. A young man,
Rhiwallon, takes his herds on occasions towards the lake and on one
occasion he watches in astonishment as a beautiful girl rises up from
the lake and sits on a rock at its edge. Rhiwallon falls in love
immediately and, hoping to win her friendship, he offers her some
bread from his lunch which she refuses. He tells his mother and she
gives him some unbaked bread which he offers the next time he sees

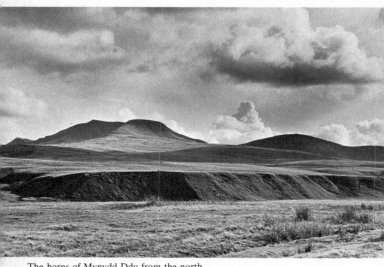

The horns of Mynydd Ddu from the north

the girl. This too she refuses but on a third occasion when his mother has given him bread baked in a different way (unleavened?), she accepts it and agrees to his proposal of marriage on the condition that her father agrees. Rhiwallon recognises that she is one of the Tylwyth Teg, the fairy folk, literally the fair people, but loving her dearly agrees to this and to the condition that she places on him should her father accept. That condition is that she will leave him if he strikes her three times. The following day Rhiwallon returns to the lake and from it emerges an old man with five daughters, all identical. The old man agrees that Rhiwallon can marry the girl provided he can pick her out from her sisters. He is dumbfounded, but the girl makes a signal with her toe so that he can choose her. Her dowry is a great number of oxen and sheep and the couple settle down to life together. Three sons are born, but over a period of time Rhiwallon does strike her three times, usually in the form of a light tap to correct what he sees as incorrect behaviour –

Llyn y fan fach from Bannau Sir Gaer

for instance, laughing at a funeral and crying at a wedding. On the third occasion she promptly returns to the lake taking with her the dowry of oxen and sheep. Since she is a good mother however she returns often to explain to her growing sons the secrets of fairy medicines, and they grow up to be fine healers and form the basis of a line of doctors stretching through history.

The story is not so greatly different from other folk tales, and even from some of the stories in the Mabinogion, but there are subtle parts to the story that suggest that it is based on not only truth, but on a quite remarkable folk memory. When the iron-using Celts first moved into Wales, in the final millennium BC, they would have encountered a people who were largely of New Stone Age culture, even if they possessed bronze implements. Such people were Mediterranean in origin and would have been short and dark-skinned, as indeed many Welsh people are today. There are several different versions of the story, though all agree on the

salient details, but in the longer and more local versions the girl's
relatives are short and dark, and they visit Rhiwallon's people's
market on occasions, though they converse in sign language as they
cannot speak his people's language. It is known that the older
culture did, on occasions, live in lake communities, on semi-floating
platforms which made it appear, perhaps, that the people could rise
out of the water. Rhiwallon has problems selecting the girl because
all foreigners look the same, and in some versions he must not strike
her with iron, a taboo that could be expected in non-iron-using
cultures. Her excellence in teaching her sons to be healers could
come from the older culture's cleverness in the use of herbal
remedies.

Seen in this light what was an old folk tale, pleasant but shallow,
becomes a remarkable tale of the touching of two cultures many
centuries ago. It would indeed be good if the story did represent the
coming of the Celts to Wales, as the implication of the story is that
the culture shock was minimal and that the Celts mingled with the
original settlers rather than destroying them out of hand, as has so
often happened in the history of advanced societies meeting
relatively backward ones.

The escarpment cliffs can give the lake an air of mystery on cold,
misty days, but in summer it is a delightful place alive with the calls
of meadow pipits parachuting to earth, and with the flashes of
sandpipers beating across the moorland. The lake water is a
breeding ground for a large number of eels, the people who
consume the two million gallons each day that it supplies being
presumably unaware that both eels and fairies inhabit their water
supply.

From the lake follow the water board road northward and
towards Llanddeusant, a hamlet whose church has some
fourteenth-century features. Before Llanddeusant, at (779246), a
track right can be followed to common land on Mynydd y llan. Go
north-east, cossing the road, to the flank of Fedw Fawr (802274).
Turning north-west we head across the moor to a path at (785285)
which is followed to Sarnau (783290). Follow the road into
Myddfai. Those who, at Llanddeusant, are interested in a change of
scenery can follow the road all the way to Myddfai. At first sight this

Bryn Poeth Uchaf
■ Youth Hostel

190

Rhandirmwyn

Old mine

1000' Hafod-y-pant

Afon Tywi

750'

500'

185

750'

Cilycwm

750'

△ (341m 1119')

Fforest

750'

500'

Llanwrtyd-Wells

A483

180

250'

Llandovery

A40 Brecon

A40

Llandeilo

1250

(173m · 568')

500'

Cefn-yr-allt-uchaf

A4069

175 Cefn-Rhuddau

Llandeilo

250' Pant-y-gaseg 500'

Pont Pwll-defaid

Myrtle Hill

Myddfai

does not seem a good option, but it is. The lanes are a delight, typical examples of what the heretic in Wales would call English country lanes!

Myddfai is the reputed home of Rhiwallon, the finest of the physician sons of the lady of the lake. Rhiwallon was named after his father and started the line of physicians in the town. This line is known to have lasted at least 600 years, and regardless of whether its actual starting was supernatural or not that is a remarkable achievement for so small a village. The first doctor known to have lived in the area was the twelfth-century physician to the local lord who was actually called Rhiwallon. For references to later members of the line it is necessary only to look at the memorials in the church, or at the local place-names. The church has many memorials to surgeons and physicians, the last being to one who died in 1842 in Aberystwyth. In the area there are farms named for the 'feddygs', physicians, Evan and Meredith, as well as a physician's gate where, reputedly, the lake lady handed her knowledge on to Rhiwallon. An interesting part of the story is the existence, in the British Museum, of a list of remedies and prescriptions written down centuries ago by the Myddfai physicians. These include some country homilies including – 'A cold mouth and warm feet will live long' and 'If thou desirest to die, eat cabbage in August'. Some of the cures are grim. To extract a tooth painlessly requires the making of a powder from newts and 'those nasty beetles which are found in ferns during summer'. This is rubbed on the offending tooth, which promptly falls out. Another involved hen's dung, gunpowder and brimstone taken as a medicine. The patient was allowed to feed normally the day after though 'tis likely he will not eat anything'! A mixture of cat's gall and hen's fat rubbed in the eyes allows one to see 'things which are invisible to others'. The tongue from a live frog laid on the heart of a sleeping man will make him confess wrongdoings in his sleep. There are also recipes for deeds that are almost witchcraft.

Myddfai is also the burial place of Morgan Owen, another of the great churchmen of Wales, who built the porch of St. Mary's church, Oxford and was chaplain to Archbishop Laud. He died in 1644.

From Myddfai take the road going west then north-west to Myrtle

Myddfai Church

Hill (767308). Here go left along the lane to Pont Pwll-defaid
(758311). Beyond the bridge go right on a minor road to a track
heading north at (761311). Follow this past Pant-y-gaseg at
(761313) to Cefn-Rhuddan at (762321). Go north again to
(763326) where a track goes east to (765326), where it turns
north-east for Cefn-yr-allt-uchaf at (768332). From here a footpath
contours around the hill to the mill at (771341), and from there a
lane leads to the road for Llandovery. This section of the route,
from Myddfai to Llandovery, has some very fine 'soft' scenery, and
is a good introduction to the joys to come as the route heads north
from the town to the plateau of Elenydd.

Elenydd

Llandovery

Llandovery has been important ever since the Roman invasion of Wales as the site lay at the intersection of several important river valleys, those of the Bran, Tywi and Gwydderig and thus on the cross-roads of highways between important forts. As a consequence there was a Roman fort here, the earthworks still remaining to the north-east of the town. In the centre of the earthworks is St. Mary's church. Since it cannot now be established as fact it must be conjecture that the fort had a temple, and that this site was maintained as a holy one after the Romans had retreated and were replaced by early Christians. It is likely therefore that St. Mary's church is the latest in the line of holy buildings that have occupied the same site for nearly 2,000 years. Now the church has a few features remaining of what was probably the earliest stone structure, the Norman building. In the main, however, it is newer, and has suffered much from restoration, though the fourteenth-century tower with its little stair-turret is largely original and very pleasant. In the churchyard is buried one of Llandovery's more famous sons, William Williams the hymn writer, whose statue stands in the Marble Hall of Cardiff's Civic Centre. Williams was born locally in 1717 and after being, briefly, a student of medicine, devoted his life to the church, initially as an Anglican curate and later as a Methodist minister. He died in 1791 and is buried on the north side of St. Mary's beneath a polished red granite obelisk which was erected at a later date. The inscribed name Williams Pantycelyn is from his home and was presumably used to distinguish him from other Williamses.

Following the departure of the Romans the site was probably abandoned, at least partially, for when Dingat, son of Prince Brychan, founded a church in the hamlet here in the fifth century it was not on the site of the Roman fort, but to the south-west of the present town centre. Prince Brychan was the first Welsh lord of this area, giving his name to it – Brycheiniog or Breconshire. In

appearance St. Dingat's is similar to St. Mary's, with its squat
embattled tower. Its history is more chequered, St. Dingat's having
been twice ruined by fire in uprisings. Later still it was badly
flooded, as was much of the town, when the Tywi burst its banks in
the seventeenth century. Many buildings were destroyed with men
and animals drowned. It was said, though not until later so perhaps
as embroidery, that the graveyard was scoured, bodies floating
away. At the time of the flood there was a man working on the
banks having guaranteed, at a price, to prevent any future flooding.
Not surprisingly he was conspicuous by his absence, as were his
banks, after the waters receded. A more permanent solution was
applied later when the river either of its own accord or with
assistance moved to a more easterly course.

That there are two churches is a curiosity and probably implies
that at one stage there were actually two parishes, Llandingat near
St. Dingat's, and Llandyfri after St. Mary's, the church on the Dyfri
as the Nant Bawddwr was then known. The latter name was
adopted for the town, the former church now being the parish
church. The name Llandovery was given to the castle that the
Normans constructed when they moved into the area. Originally the
Normans used the Roman fortification adding a motte that can still
be seen – St. Mary's church stands on it – but the site was
unsatisfactory as its perimeter was too large to hold successfully
with limited soldiers, and so another castle was built to the south.
This was taken and retaken in various skirmishes for about 150
years and then sacked by Owain Glyndwr. Now only the remnants
of the keep remain. These are on private land owned by the *Castle
Hotel* from which permission to view may be obtained.

During the course of the Glyndwr revolt the town saw some of
the brutality of the conflict at first hand. As mentioned earlier
Glyndwr sacked the castle, but that was after Henry IV had used it
on his first march into Wales in 1400. As an early attempt to stop
the revolt getting out of hand Henry had one Llywelyn ap Grufydd
Fychan, a local landowner, hanged, drawn and quartered in the
market square. His crime was that his sons were believed to be with
Owain. Since Owain's sacking of the castle also included the firing

of the town and the killing of some inhabitants the Llandovery townsfolk must have felt that a third opinion was what was required. Less than one hundred years later another local was in trouble with the English Royal House. This time it was the lord, Rhys ap Gruffydd or Rhys fitz Urien as he liked to be called, believing himself to be descended from Urien, a knight of King Arthur. Rhys was a champion of Katherine of Aragon in her fight to avoid divorce and thus did not endear himself to Anne Boleyn. Once in power she persuaded Henry VIII that Rhys's love of the name Urien concealed a love of the name Arthur, Henry's brother, meaning a dislike of Henry and a desire for Welsh sovereignty. This is tortured logic by any standards but it worked, and Rhys was beheaded for treason.

Following this century of unpleasantness Llandovery settled down to quiet prosperity assisted by its fairs and twice-weekly markets. This peaceable existence allowed the established religions to flourish. The Nonconformists arrived and set up meetings in a local cave, and Rhys Prichard became town vicar. Prichard was a man of absolute piety, forever pointing out the iniquities of his flock, and writing a book of religious verse, the *Welshman's Candle*, for which he is renowned. It appears likely that his uncompromising piety and total honesty were the reasons that the story of his drunkenness became rife after his death. It is almost as though the man was so good that folk had to invent a little badness to prevent themselves being blinded by the light. There was a saying among Llandovery folk, according to George Borrow writing nearly 200 years later, that 'bad we may be but not half as bad as the parson'. But Borrow also noted that 200 years later Prichard was still known as *The* Vicar. Prichard was buried in St. Dingat's churchyard, but the site of his grave is not known.

War having been the problem during Llandovery's early years, it is ironic that it was war that led to a sharp increase in prosperity in the late eighteenth century. The European war was preventing England from receiving meat from the continent, and so the driving of Welsh animals to England, a trade that had been established since early times, increased dramatically. The droving trade will be mentioned again farther north when a drove-road is briefly

The main square, Llandovery

followed. In the trade Llandovery was of considerable importance.

It was a large town, by the standards of the day, with many inns, strategically placed at fords and valley heads, and to help overcome the problem of robbery a Llandovery man set up one of the first banks. This was the Black Ox Bank, the Ox appearing on receipts and cheques, and made the town very popular with those drovers anxious to retain some of their cash. The droving business provided prosperity not only to the innkeepers, but to a host of townsfolk whose trade depended on the cattle, the skinners and leather-tanners, the saddlers and glove-makers.

The same geographical factors that led to Llandovery's importance as a droving station also led to its becoming a coaching station. The prosperity derived from droving and coaching continued when the railway put an end to both trades because Llandovery's position meant it was still important as a meeting and market town, and since a railway station was placed here what it lost on one hand it gained on the other. The prosperity is reflected in the architecture of the town with its collection of late Georgian buildings. Especially fine is the town hall completed in 1858 and incorporating an open market hall at one end. It is an imposing structure which is the fourth in a line of halls on the site. The immediate predecessor of this hall was a building somewhat lacking in charm if the records are to be believed for it was not only a crumbling ruin but required the town council to pay 2s. 6d. to Ebenezer Thomas, the butcher, occasionally for use of his dog to kill rats. Elsewhere in the square, the *King's Head* and the original Market Hall with its clock tower are worthy of note, and other houses in Broad Street and High Street make a quiet walk around the town very worthwhile.

Gone now are the days of the early nineteenth century when visitors to Llandovery found it less than endearing. Malkin found 'its buildings are mean, irregular and unconnected; its streets filthy and disgusting', and a little later someone thought the town had 'nothing to recommend it . . . a few straggling streets generally extremely dirty'. When George Borrow came 50 years later he was enchanted. On leaving he wrote, 'I have no hesitation in saying (Llandovery) is about the pleasantest little town in which I have halted in the course of my wanderings.'

Unfortunately we too must leave Llandovery. The route followed depends as much upon the wayfarer's method of accommodation as upon anything else at this stage. Youth hostellers making for the hostel east of the Rhandirmwyn may go along the minor road that leaves the A483 at (771354) going north via (783407) and (783419) for Hafod-y-pant (800432) where the warden lives. It is obviously a matter of choice but the route that follows the lanes from (761348) or (767347) along the Tywi valley towards Rhandirmwyn seems preferable as it offers very fine views up the valley. A visit may be made to Cilycwm, which is a picturesque village, with cobbled edges to its street, grouped around a fine fifteenth-century church restored with taste early this century and containing an original family box pew. There are also several nonconformist chapels, including a tiny Baptist chapel in keeping with the compact nature of this delightful spot.

It is to Rhandirmwyn, however, that the wayfarer is travelling and the history of the area around the village comes as a great surprise.

Despite the image that Wales, other than the valleys, now conveys, of a largely agriculturally based country, historically the country has always been important industrially. This is largely due to its enormous mineral wealth. Lately this has meant slate and coal, but in earlier days, when industry was on a more piecemeal basis and production was limited, it also meant metal mining. At times when the need for expensive metals, and even iron, was small Wales was a prospector's paradise. There were lead mines in every one of the old Welsh counties, gold in Carmarthenshire and Merionethshire, most particularly in the area around Dolgellau, and copper in Anglesey and Caernarvonshire, with Parys mountain in Anglesey being a famous site.

The largest mine in Carmarthenshire, indeed in the whole of South Wales, was here at Rhandirmwyn. Indeed the name means mining district, the site itself being called Nantymwyn from the position of the main shafts on the banks of the Nant y Bai, which drains the hills to the south of Llyn Brianne down into the Afon Tywi. The mining was spread over a wide area, as it occurred over a long period, and the wayfarer coming upon the remains suddenly is somewhat taken aback by the sight of industrial spoil in this, one of the most peaceful and secluded valleys in the whole of Wales. It is difficult to be precise about times in some of the Welsh mines as it is possible that minor workings existed in Roman times, but by 1775 the mine was being worked in earnest, and very profitably. A fine watercolour by Warwick Smith, now in the National Library of Wales, Aberystwyth, shows the surface workings of the mine in 1792, as dated, with a large waterwheel beside a small number of buildings. It is likely that the waterwheel was the power in an ore-crushing house, the remains of a stack indicating that at a later stage the wheel was replaced by a steam engine. As much as 4,000 tons of ore were raised annually at the time of highest output. The site was never served by tram or railway, the ore being moved in donkey-borne panniers, at first to Carmarthen and later to Llanelli. The mine continued to be worked despite the difficulties this caused, but it became increasingly unprofitable. Various attempts were made in the early twentieth century to mine successfully, but they all failed to a greater or lesser extent, and after 1937 no further attempt was made. An investigation of the plans of shafts and levels reveals that the mine contained Upper and Lower Boat Levels, the reason being that the difficulties of draining the flooded levels became too great on occasions and they were allowed to stay flooded, the miners traversing them by boat to continue work on the dry side.

The village of Rhandirmwyn itself is a showpiece, a delightful collection of houses which belies its largely industrial background. From it continue up the Tywi valley, which is becoming increasingly excellent to the point (772459) at which the road divides with Troedrhiw signed off left and Llyn Brianne off right. There is a small choice to be made here. The wayfarer, if he is not going to the Youth Hostel at Ty'n-y-Cornel, will be heading for Soar Chapel (784533). The best way is unquestionably to go up the Doethie valley, a route which is shorter and goes through some of the finest scenery in mid-Wales. The longer route goes along the road to Llyn Brianne and then follows its eastern shore through the forestry plantations to Soar. It has some interesting points and is worthy of consideration by anyone who has followed the Doethie previously.

The first point of interest, a cave, can be reached by following the

track through woodland from (782463). This is the cave of Twm
Shon Catti. He was born at the end of the sixteenth century to
unmarried Catherine Jones of Tregaron and she named him
Thomas John. Because he had no surname he became known to the
locals as Cathy's Tom John, or Twm Shon Catti in Welsh. Twm
grew up to become the Welsh equivalent of Robin Hood, though
with more humour and less tragedy than accompanied the English
outlaw.

Continuing along the road the wayfarer reaches Llyn Brianne.
This is an artificial lake, a reservoir behind a thoroughly modern
dam nearly 300 feet high. The flooding of the area may have been,
at the time, a tragedy, but there is no denying the beauty that has
been created by the lake. The natural advantages of the lake, and of
the dam itself which has a stark beauty, enhanced considerably by
the 'flip-bucket' water discharge which causes a fountain of water
(of the same appearance but considerably bigger than those that
hold up golf balls at fun fairs) that sparkles in the sun causing its
own rainbow, have been carefully stage-managed, with car parks
and viewing points.

The way to Soar is now a straightforward and pleasant, if long,
trek through the woodland of Towy forest, around the shores of the
lake.

The better route takes the road to Troedrhiw, a road that follows
one bank and then the other of the Doethie river. This is delightful
country, one of the very best valleys in mid-Wales with good views
all around. Indeed this entire section from south of Rhandirmwyn,
approaching the head of the Tywi valley and then taking the narrow
valley of a tributary, is one of the better lowland sections on the
whole journey from Cardiff to Conwy. The road we are on now is an
old drove-road and it would be good to think that the drovers chose
this way as much for its aesthetic qualities as for its speed.

The drovers performed in the Middle Ages the job that brought
fame to the cowboys of the mid-west in the nineteenth century. The
first drovers were probably pre-Norman, but it became an
established practice in Norman times and continued until the
nineteenth century when better transport brought the trade to an
end. The herds were generally taken over the barren mountain ways

Looking north towards Rhandirmwyn

so that the crop-lands were not interfered with, and their progress
can occasionally be noted by the siting of a *Butcher's Arms*, animals
being slaughtered en route to provide local meat supplies. Unlike
the mid-west droves it was not only cattle that came. Then, as now,
the sheep was the chief animal of upland Wales, but there were also
pigs and geese and later turkeys as well. A large drove must have
been a spectacular sight. Together with the animals were the
drovers, of course, and many other travellers, for Wales was a wild
place and there was safety in numbers. The drovers worked hard on
the big herds and relaxed on the way back, taking a coach perhaps
and the occasional night at an inn. If they managed to avoid being
robbed they probably arrived back broke in time to drive again.

We travel in the footsteps, or should it be hoof-marks, of the
drovers and their herds back up the Doethie valley to (771514)
where paths go on up the valley and right, the drove-road, to

The 'flip bucket', Llyn Brianne

Soar-y-mynydd chapel. Youth hostellers carrying on here may not, in fact, visit the chapel as they may receive permission at the hostel to move northwards from (742543) to the mountain road at (762576). The right of way goes right to Soar, the loneliest chapel in Wales to which worshippers came on horse-back, and from there by lane – it is hardly a road – to the same point. From here the true Elenydd is crossed.

Elenydd

The name Elenydd is an ancient one. Giraldus Cambrensis uses it to describe the whole of the mountain area of South Wales, as opposed to Eryri, the mountains of North Wales. However, since Giraldus also named Plynlimon, and recognised the sandstone masses of what is now the Brecon Beacons National Park, he clearly meant by Elenydd that area between Plynlimon and Mynydd Ddu. Giraldus claims the area was called, in English, Moruge, though there appears little justification for such a claim. It is likely that the name derives from the Afon Elan to the north of the area, but it is such a delightful name that it seems fitting to apply it to the entire high plateau area north of the Tywi valley and Rhandirmwyn and south of the Wye valley and of Plynlimon. The eastern part of this area is the Welsh lake district, a series of reservoirs having been created by the damming of the rivers that flowed in the wide valleys. The first, as we have seen, is Llyn Brianne. To the north are the Claerwen and then the reservoirs of the Elan valley. It is an arguable point whether Welsh valleys should be flooded to provide the industrial Midlands of England with water, and any extension of the reservoirs should be viewed cautiously, at least. Since the Elan valley dams were completed in the early years of this century and the Claerwen in the early fifties the author can claim, by reason of age, to be only capable of assessing the reservoirs as they are, not by a comparison with the unflooded valleys. In that context the water is attractive at a distance, but somewhat sterile, the lack of tree cover at the edges of Claerwen and Craig Goch meaning that the reservoirs do not have the secretive, cool beauty of Lake Vyrnwy to the north, or even Llyn Brianne for that matter.

However, the route suggested stays to the west of the big reservoirs, visiting instead small pools that are dark and forbidding and generate a considerable atmosphere. The pools lie above Strata Florida, and from Rhandirmwyn there are 15 miles of quite magnificent moorland to be crossed. The wilderness lover could hardly be better served, the lover of scenic beauty could hardly improve on the valleys of Gwenffrwd, Pysgotwr and Doethie, and for the nature lover there is the red kite. The kite is the most famous and sought-after of Welsh raptors, though it is probable that the goshawk of Snowdonia, the hen harrier and even perhaps the peregrine falcon are rarer. But with its beautiful chestnut colour and deeply forked tail it is one of the finest of British birds. Though the bird is a moorland feeder it nests in trees, and the wooded valleys north of Rhandirmwyn are potential nest sites. The bird is a nervous nester and any disturbance can cause it to desert its eggs or chicks. The loss of a brood would be a disaster, and the pestering of the bird at nest cannot be tolerated. It is likely that the wayfarer will take two days to reach Cwmystwyth. During the whole of that time he may see the bird working the ridges on the moor, so there is no need to go searching for it. The author once saw three at once to the north-east of Ffair Rhos, and one above the main road to the south of the Rheidol valley, so there is considerable scope for viewing.

Our route leads northwards across the moorland. This section is a very real test of navigational ability, and the wayfarer should consider very carefully before embarking on a crossing if the weather is poor and visibility limited. The route starts easily enough along the track to Nant y Maen (761585), but beyond that there is no real path and the ground can be marshy, particularly in wet weather. In good weather or, rather, in good visibility, this section of the route, and that to the north of Strata Florida over similar terrain, are very fine, even beautiful if the walker's idea of beauty extends to weather-beaten moorland offering, at best, solitude, at worst loneliness. There are no real landmarks, but the top of Garn Gron (740611) can be a haven to the traveller who is a little bewildered. It must be borne in mind, however, that the summit is actually right in the middle of nowhere. North of Garn Gron the walker goes west of the crags of Carn Fflur (743625) to discover that there is now forestry down to grid line 63. This does nothing to improve the navigation, indeed far from it because the trees cut down the view considerably. The wayfarer is making for Talwrn (745649), a dangerous ruin, but useful landmark. From it an obvious track leads down to the abbey of Strata Florida (746657), the latter part of which includes some paddling as a stream has been diverted down the pathway.

Strata Florida

The remains of Strata Florida are not extensive but the pastoral setting, on the banks of the Teifi river, is wonderfully peaceful. Strangely the name derives not from the river, but from the Latin form of the Welsh Ystrad Fflur, the valley of the Afon Fflur that also runs into Tregaron Bog, parallel to, but 2 miles south of, the Teifi. The reason is that the abbey was originally sited 2 miles to the south-west in a field still called Yr Hen Fynachlog, the old monastery.

Bryn
Dafydd   225   Llyn Fyrddon-
                             Fawr

Llyn
Fyrddon-
Fach   (593m △
              1945')   Llyn Du
                             1750'

↑ Pontrhydygroes/
  Devil's Bridge

B4343
                                          1500'

Ffair Rhos
                                          1500'

                                          Teifi Pools

                        Afon Teifi

                   (459m   220
                    1500')

Pontrhydfendigaid
                                    1250'
Strata Florida   1000'

on
                   St Mary's Abbey
B4343   750'   Tyn-y-cwm   Dibyn
                                                         Du
Tregaron   215

                Talwrn
                        1000'

                        ↑

          1250'   Carn Fflur

              1500'
Garn Gron   Llyn
△   Crugnant
(541m
1775')   210

                        1500'
                   Nant y Maen

                   1250'

The Normans, while not having invented the monastic house, certainly did an enormous amount to promote the idea of monasticism. Many Norman lords gave land and money for house-building, and lands for the upkeep of the house and monks. All of the great houses, Benedictine, Cistercian, Franciscan, were of Continental origin and while the English, that is Saxons, readily absorbed the houses into the landscape and culture the Welsh were more suspicious: the foreign houses seemed too attached to the Normans. The founding of the abbey is generally ascribed to Robert Fitzstephen who held large tracts of West Wales, and the agreed date is around 1160, some 100 years after the Conquest. That such a benefaction was fraught with danger can be deduced from the fact that within two years Rhys ap Gruffydd had attacked Norman Cardiganshire, conquering the whole district and taking Robert Fitzstephen prisoner. The house Fitzstephen had founded was Cistercian which extolled the virtues of simplicity, hard work in agriculture and extreme poverty. It seems that the quiet dignity of the house won Rhys over, a charter of 1184 naming him as builder of the abbey. In fact the building of the abbey seems to have occupied a very long period, the Chapter House having been completed only in 1235, the bell only being brought in 1254. The bell is of interest as its purchase price was 97 marks and two cows.

Despite its Norman foundations the abbey became, perhaps because of its remoteness from England, the centre of Welsh influence, and a great cultural centre also. When Llywelyn Fawr of Gwynedd decided to assemble Welsh lords and princes together to swear their allegiance to his son Dafydd, it was to Strata Florida that he called them in 1238. It is said that within the cemetery many of these princes and also princes from later ages are buried. Because of this association with Welsh nationalism, the abbey has been called the Welsh Westminster. It fared badly in the rebellion of Owain Glyndwr, for in 1401 when the army of Henry IV was being harried by the guerilla fighters of the Welsh prince a baggage train belonging to his young son, Henry, Prince of Wales, was attacked and robbed. King Henry was furious and marched on Strata Florida. There he and his knights released the pent-up frustrations of the failing Welsh campaign in a blasphemous fury. The abbey was

Norman archway, St. Mary's Abbey, Strata Florida

plundered, its holy vessels stolen, its buildings looted, and many monks were murdered. Henry ordered that the horses should be tethered at the high altar, with inevitable consequences for the church. His knights drank the abbey's wine cellars dry in a two-day spree, then smashed down the buildings and fired the ruins. In later life Henry is reported to have been in an agony of conscience over the acts, though this must have been much later as his son quartered an army here in 1407 during the siege of Aberystwyth castle. The holiness of the spot meant that when peace returned the abbey was rebuilt, and was in constant occupation up until the time of dissolution.

Despite the ravages suffered by the abbey in the early fifteenth century, and a fire following a lightning strike in the late thirteenth century, there is a considerable amount of Norman work in the abbey including a superb Norman doorway. Not much else of the structure remains intact. Following dissolution the abbeys were customarily stripped of their roofs and over a period of time the walls collapsed, a decay assisted by locals who used the abbeys as a convenient quarry for building stone. As a consequence little remains that is immediately discernible to the layman. Nevertheless the site still has a quiet dignity.

As mentioned before, the abbey cemetery is the burial place of many of the early princes of the territories of Wales. The church cemetery beside it was the burial place of Dafydd ap Gwilym, the greatest of medieval Welsh poets who was buried here in the latter part of the fourteenth century. Traditionally Dafydd was buried under the yew tree, though the memorials to him are very recent. He was born at Penrhyncoch near Aberystwyth and is renowned for his prose poems on all subjects from love to humour. He is especially fine at describing the natural world. His liking for humour suggests that Dafydd would have liked the memorial erected near his yew tree in 1756. The tombstone was incised with a leg to the thigh, the inscription reading 'The leg and part of the thigh of Henry Hughes, Cooper, was cut off and interred here June 18th 1756'. Hughes was injured in a stage coach crash, but survived and prospered well enough to emigrate to the USA on his one leg.

The yew tree above the grave of Dafydd ap Gwilym, Strata Florida

From the abbey ruins take the lane going eastward to Ty'n-y-cwm (771655) from where a path leads back onto the moorland of Elenydd.

To the north-east from here are the Teifi pools where there is some of the wildest and loneliest, but at the same time loveliest, country of Elenydd. The land here is grassland, one of the few remaining areas in Wales of grass moor, as opposed to rough or peat moor, left unpolluted by ranks of conifers. It is a land of great beauty with a flora that could keep the most difficult to please flower-lover busy for some time, and again the chance of seeing kites. The pools feed the Teifi river that then flows into Cors Tregaron, Tregaron Bog, a grade 1 naturalist site where many rare bog plants grow and insects abound, and where in winter the ducks attract a fine assortment of raptors including the hen harrier. In summer the great grey shrike makes an occasional visit.

The Teifi pools were the scene, in 1929, of a tragedy when an old tramp who had left Ffair Rhos was caught here in a blizzard. Then, as now, this was a place of little shelter, and he died of cold and exposure. Not until the snow cleared several weeks later was the body discovered. A search of his body for some identification revealed 8½d. but no name. The farmers and villagers of Ffair Rhos were troubled by the sadness of the incident and money was found for a burial at Strata Florida. On a slab stone a local carved the epitaph –

UNKNOWN
He died upon the hillside drear
Alone where snow was deep
By strangers he was carried here
Where princes also sleep.

It is a sobering thought, particularly if the mist comes down and the temperature drops. There is now an escape road to Ffair Rhos to the west and, though longer, to Claerwen to the east. Ahead is a 5-mile stretch of relatively featureless moorland, the sensible route to Cwmystwyth being to head off to the Fyrddon lakes, to follow them and then to go north. Strictly this route is not on a right of

Mining spoil, Cwmystwyth

way, but public access was guaranteed at the time Birmingham Water Works was granted permission to create reservoirs in the Elan valley to the east. The old mining ruins east of Cwmystwyth are worth visiting and can be reached directly by the intrepid stream-crosser or by the bridges, one at Cwmystwyth itself, one farther east.

Cwmystwyth

Cwmystwyth represents perhaps the most tangible sign of Cardiganshire's mineral wealth, the deserted mine buildings and spoil heaps littering the valley of the Afon Ystwyth for several hundred yards. It is a paradise for the mining historian and industrial archaeologist, but even for the casual visitor it is a powerful site. While on the one hand, and from the aesthetic point of view, the site is a desolation, a vandalising of a beautiful river valley, and a dangerous vandalism at that, on the other hand the creaking doors, the wind in the old buildings, the ghosts of past presences, lend an air of mystery and a link with a richer lode of life. Despite the ruins the site is an empty and lonely one, and the wayfarer who visits alone and wanders through it will experience an isolation which does not exist to the same intensity on the lonely moorland to the south.

It was noted, in 1872, that the mine was 'both the richest and the oldest wrought mine in the county (of Cardiganshire), having produced considerably more than two million sterling of lead ore.' That is an enormous financial profit, and represents, in ore terms, the mining of, probably, in excess of 100,000 tons of rock. The reasons for the richness is that the site is above not one but a dozen or so lodes, not only of lead but of copper. The area has certainly been worked since earliest times as stone tools have been found on Copper Hill to the east of the main workings. The name is interesting as it appears to have been given to the hill quite specifically, but is entered on the Ordnance Survey maps as Copa Hill. Since 'copa' is Welsh for crest, or top, a term which could only marginally be applied to the hill, and not for copper, it is perhaps an example of an English name 'welshised' as opposed to a Welsh one Anglicised. The hill was later mined by the scouring technique applied, as we have seen, to expose coal and ironstone at Blaenavon. Here the technique was called hushing and has produced a series of radiating gashes from an old reservoir on the hill above the Nant yr Onen stream. It is believed by many experts to represent the finest example of the technique in Britain, though in purely aesthetic terms it can hardly be said to enhance the beauty of the valley of the small stream.

The earliest workings of the lodes were by the cutting of open trenches or by the boring of adits. An adit was a shaft that entered the hillside horizontally or, in practice, sloping upwards slightly, so that water collecting at the mining point drained away naturally. Drainage was a problem which was always encountered in Welsh mineral mines, and is of course a problem of mines generally. Before the invention of the water pump, or any successful method of powering such a pump over the large distances required, it

Mining ruin, Cwmystwyth

represented the simplest solution. Later when waterwheels and then steam engines were sited to pump water the adit levels were used as drains. At the end of the adit the lode was worked in stopes, levels cut out from the adit into the ore-bearing rock. When the lodes at surface level were exhausted and water pumping was feasible, shafts were sunk vertically. The adit working method had allowed the ore to be removed straightforwardly, ore carts being run on rails, but vertical shafts required hand or horse powered windings and, later, winding frames similar to those used at collieries. The ore was then lifted out in a kibble, a bucket-type carrier. Some separation of metal and metal concentrate from rock took place at the site in order to reduce the carriage.

At one stage the main shafts were drained by a waterwheel 30 feet in diameter. The waterwheel is a grand machine, the one at Llywernog farther north being, at 50 feet, a superb specimen. The impression of size and grandeur is enhanced when the wheels are set, as was the customary mining practice, not hard against mill buildings but in wheelpits. Not only the device itself, but some of the statistics associated with it, are astonishing. For a 40-foot diameter over-shot wheel, that is, one in which the water ran over the wheel, producing a working power of 25 h.p. continuously, the daily water requirement was a staggering 6 million gallons. Such a consumption would lower the level of a 10-acre pond by about $2\frac{1}{2}$ feet!

The mine itself closed in 1921, since when the site has been picked over by visitors, archaeologists and the wind. Though it will never be as it was before mining started it is very gradually returning to the natural state.

From Cwmystwyth village take the track opposite the chapel (786743) to houses and on north to another house at (786748). From here care is needed to follow a pathway through to the road at (783751). Go right and then left on a forest track to Gelmast (776756) and continue on to the B4574 at The Arch (765756) erected in 1810 to celebrate the Golden Jubilee of George III's accession. Here go right and then left off the road on a track that leads straightforwardly to the B4343 at (738764). Go right and down to Devil's Bridge.

Devil's Bridge

Devil's Bridge is the first of the 'honeypots' that the wayfarer meets on his journey northward. There will be others and the traveller should think deeply before shunning such spots. There is much here that is truly delightful, even if some of it is enclosed by wire and visited only by those with the right coin to operate the turnstile rather than those intrepid enough to brave the ravine. The system calls to mind the story of the traveller in America who stayed at a hotel close to a particularly beautiful gorge. A pathway to, and a viewpoint of, the scene had been beaten to the spot and there the visitor was confronted by a sign that read 'View by kind permission of – Hotel' to which someone had added 'with just a little help from God'.

The river at this point is the Afon Mynach, or Monk's river, as the abbey of Strata Florida owned sheep grazing lands in the area. It

was the monks from Strata Florida who built the first, and lowest (of course!), of the bridges over the ravine. This bridge was built in 1087, and looks as usable now, in theory only, as it was 900 years ago. The bridge also gave the spot its true name, Pontarfynach. The name Devil's Bridge is derived from the Welsh Pont-y-gwr-drwg, roughly the bridge of the evil one, which is from a legend regarding the establishment of the first bridge. The legend concerns Marged, an old woman who lived in a cottage close to the edge of the ravine. Marged's sole source of income was her cow, Malen, whom she milked daily, milk that was sold to her neighbours. One morning Marged went out to milk Malen after a night of particularly heavy rain to discover that the cow had crossed the river above the ravine and was now marooned on the far side by the raging torrent. Marged was beside herself as not milking Malen would not only mean no money but also that the cow would suffer. Standing at the edge of the ravine she called out in despair that she would give anything for a bridge to cross it. Immediately a voice answered saying that he would build her a bridge, and looking up Marged saw a figure in the white habit and cowl of a Strata Florida Cistercian monk on the far side. The cowl over his head seemed curiously shaped and he was turned so that his face did not show, but despite this, and the fact that she could hear him clearly over the roar of the water, Marged was so heartened that she asked how long it might take. Just an hour, said the monk, provided that he was allowed to take the first living thing that crossed it. In her excitement Marged took little notice of his final proviso and hurried back to her cottage, the monk having told her that she must not witness the miraculous bridge building. At the cottage she ate a hurried breakfast and at last she heard the monk's voice calling her. She rushed back to the ravine still holding a bread crust, and accompanied by her dog. There was indeed a bridge across the ravine and on the far side was the monk holding Malen. Marged started to cross but at that instant the monk's cowl slipped slightly and Marged saw that its curious shape was due to the monk having horns. Instantly she realised that it was the Devil in disguise, and that he was after her soul.

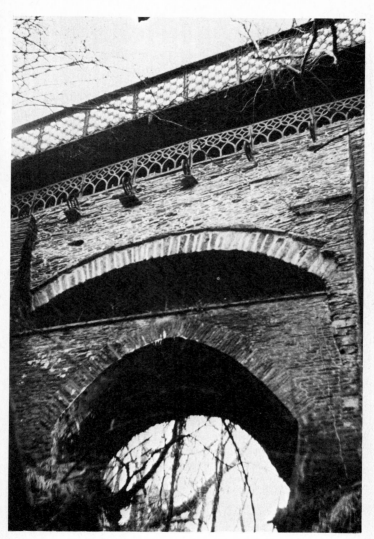

The bridges at Devil's Bridge

She was a wily old lady, however, and so she hesitated, staring at
the bridge. The Devil, impatient for her soul, asked why and she
replied that the bridge did not seem strong enough to carry her crust
of bread let alone herself. The Devil told her to throw it and see, if
she felt that way, but instead Marged threw the crust right across the
bridge and her dog immediately followed it, becoming the first
living thing to cross it. Furious the Devil disappeared in a cloud of
sulphurous smoke leaving Marged to cross the bridge and to be
re-united with Malen and the dog.

The triple bridge structure gives some idea of the advance of
bridge-building techniques. As the span length increased so the
bridge moved up towards the top of the ravine. The second bridge
was built over the first in 1708, while the top bridge is modern.
Beneath the bridges are the Mynach falls and the Devil's
Punchbowl, for which the site is so justly renowned. The Punchbowl
is on the southern side of the bridge, where the continuous torrent
has carved an elegantly smooth hollow from the mountainside. To
the north of the bridges a pathway descends 300 feet on the eastern
side of the river, crosses it and follows it closely on the ascent side to
view the magnificent falls themselves. The path involves a steep
section known, with little imagination, as Jacob's ladder, which has
been known to stop the elderly. At the top of the climb is the *Hafod
Arms Hotel*, the 'immense lofty cottage with projecting eaves'
where George Borrow stayed when visiting the gorge. Borrow
described the scene with the awe-struck horror that seemed to be
the requirement of visitors of the period. The Punchbowl becomes
'a frightful cavity (where) the waters . . . whirl, boil and hiss in a
horrid pot or cauldron . . . in a manner truly tremendous'. The
waters then escape through 'a gloomy volcanic slit'. Borrow
suggested that after seeing the Punchbowl, not the name he used as
he called it by the local name of Twll yn y graig, the hole in the cliff,
and the 'spectral, shadowy Devil's Bridge', you should 'repair to
your inn, and have no more sight-seeing that day, for you have seen
enough'! Neither would he come to terms with the falls themselves
which 'is thundering beside you; foam, foam, foam is flying all about
you; the basin . . . is boiling frightfully below you', together with
'rocks . . . frowning terribly on you' and 'forest trees, dank and wet

with spray and mist'. It would be so interesting to find out if Borrow really did find it so bad, or whether the time (he was in Wales around 1855) and his intended audience coloured his perception. For the modern wayfarer it is all of these horrid, frightful things that are so attractive, and he can handle them in quantities in excess of one per day.

Interestingly Borrow does not mention the legend of Marged and the Devil, but he does mention a story centred on a cave, now no longer visible as such, at the base of the falls. Here, he says, lived the Plant de Bat, or children of Bat, a local man. These, two boys and a girl, were notorious locally as petty thieves and they lived in the cave. One day they killed a gentleman while robbing him, and his friends sought them out, destroying the cave so they could no longer use it. The boys were hanged and the girl burnt at the stake.

To continue from the Devil's Bridge go west along the A4120 until a path leads off right (north) at (735770). Follow this to and across the railway. This is the Vale of Rheidol railway, the only steam railway operated by British Rail. It runs from Aberystwyth to the terminus at Devil's Bridge. Though not, perhaps, having the charm of the Festiniog railway, nor the dramatic impact of the Tal-y-llyn railway at Abergynolwyn, the Rheidol is a fine track, better than the other 'great little trains'. The Rheidol is a fine valley and is well seen on this short walk along it. The path drops down to the river, crossing it by a bridge. Turn right (east) and go back up river. A track is reached at (734777) that goes north through a Forestry Commission plantation towards Ystumtuen but though this is convenient it is not a right of way, that going farther south-east and east before going back north to Ystumtuen.

The wayfarer is now seeking to reach Dyffryn Castell for access to Plynlimon. From Ystumtuen the route leads north to Tyr-hir (738789). Here a path leads off east which can be followed to Parson's Bridge. Beyond the bridge is a very ancient church which had no resident vicar, one riding up the Rheidol from Aberystwyth to take services. As the original bridge was only a plank he tied his mount here, at the parson's bridge. The church is set near some ancient standing stones that have led some to believe that it was deliberately set up within a henge site that may have had some

Nant-y-moch reservoir from the high point of Plynlimon

contemporary pagan significance. Alternatively a track going north
from this one to Bryn Bras can be followed, this leading to the
footbridge at (745804) and on into Ponterwyd. Whichever path is
used the wayfarer reaches (752807) where a path leads from the
main A4120 to the B4343 which is followed to Dyffryn Castell.

An alternative to this route is to go along the lane from
Ystumtuen to the A44. To the left at this point the wayfarer can
visit another mining site, but not here a site of great importance or
great atmosphere. In fact the Llywernog lead mine was somewhat
insignificant in actual mining terms, but it has now been turned into
a museum of the industry, in spectacular style. There are several
waterwheels on site, complete specimens having been brought in to
augment the site wheel. Close to one of the wheels are a pair of
round buddles, sedimentation pools for the recovery of fine
particles of lead that had escaped from the jiggers. The jiggers were

a series of washing tubs in which the heavy lead-ore sank away from
the lighter waste. The jiggers are here also, housed in the jigger
shed. It is one of the joys of the history of mining that so many
words like buddle and jigger were used. In addition the visitor can
walk into the Plynlimon mountain as far as a pool that is, in fact, a
water-filled shaft, the shaft having been driven at the end of the
nineteenth century.

The wayfarer, whether he has visited Llywernog or not, goes east
along the A44 to Ponterwyd. Here he could go left on the minor
road to the Nant-y-moch reservoir, breaking out right from this on
to the flank of Plynlimon, or he could go on to Dyffryn Castell, by
path from the A4120 at (752807) to the B4343. At Dyffryn the lane
beside the inn is taken out on to Plynlimon.

Plynlimon

In the Mabinogion the Welsh Arthurian knights Kei and Bedwyr,
later Anglicised to Kay and Bedivere, are one day 'sitting on
Pumlumon, in the greatest wind in the world'. Later another
traveller visited the spot and declared it a 'sodden weariness'.
Accept the truth of either, or more especially of both, statements,
and you would be disinclined to visit at all. You would be wrong. It
may be a huge mass rather than a shapely group of peaks but
Plynlimon is still a fine place with excellent walking. The name is a
corruption of Pumlumon. The first syllable is certainly from 'pump',
five, but what of the rest? There is no clear-cut answer; it could be
from five rivers as five at least can be counted, but it is more likely
to mean five peaks for, with a little imagination, there can be
distinguished five tops around Llyn Llygad Rheidol. The summit of
Pen Pumlumon Fawr, the highest peak, just fails to make 2,500 feet
which is sad, but what it lacks in inches it makes up for in other ways
as it is well protected by bogs and difficult ground and affords from
its trig. or shelter fine views of the route to date over Elenydd and of
delights to come, as well as a very fine view of the spidery
Nant-y-moch reservoir not so very far below. Almost due east of
the summit, and about ¾ mile away, is the source of the river Wye,
while a couple of miles north-east is Blaenhafren, the source of the
Severn, here the Hafren.

To continue descend north from the summit to the 'standing stones' marked on the O.S. sheet, at (783895). Two stones were said to have been set up to mark the site of the first battle fought by Owain Glyndwr in his bid to create a Wales independent of England, and two are shown by the Ordnance Survey, though only a single white slab appears unnatural. Glyndwr's campaign will be dealt with in greater depth when we reach his 'capital' at Machynlleth, but the battle is worthy of note. In 1401 Glyndwr had amassed a small army of about 400 men here at the Hyddgen valley. At the time there was, in South Wales, a strong Flemish community whose lifestyle and affluence depended on English support. They were concerned that the revolt should be nipped in the bud and sent men to support a small English force. This army, about 1,500 strong, found the Welsh in this secluded valley, surrounded them and poured in on to them. Robert Vaughan, a contemporary, wrote of the battle – 'They hemmed him (Glyndwr) in on all sides so that he could not possibly get off without fighting at a great disadvantage. He and his men fought manfully a great while, in their own defence, against them. Finding themselves surrounded and hard put to it, they resolved at length to make their way through or perish in the attempt; so, falling on furiously, with courage whetted with despair they put the enemy, after a sharp dispute, to confusion; and they pursued so eagerly their advantage, that they bade them give ground, and in the end to fly outright, leaving 200 of their men dead on the spot of the engagement. This victory rendered Owain considerable renown and was the means to bring many to his side, that his number was greatly increased.'

To reach Machynlleth continue up the Hyddgen valley and then go west of the forest to the head of Cregiau Bwlch-Hyddgen (766935). From here the choices are endless. The wayfarer can go down to the road at (775960) and follow it to Machynlleth, a good route despite the tarmac. Alternatively go northward to the bridleway at (766956) and follow it to Bwlch (755975). Continue on the bridleway that goes north through the forest east of Glanmerin lake, and at the wood edge (757994) go north to the golf course and minor road. At the road go left and enter Machynlleth.

Machynlleth

About a mile to the south-west of the Clock Tower which stands in
the centre of Machynlleth are a series of steps leading to an area of
common land on Wylfa hill. The steps are known as the Roman
steps as local legend claims they were built by the Romans as access
to their frontier post on Wylfa hill itself. The legend also includes a
further post at Bryn-y-Gog, now a housing estate in the
north-eastern corner of the town, to back up the known Roman
occupation of a fort at Pennal. A thousand years later the position
of the town, near a crossing of the Dovey and at the mouths of
valleys going north and south both of which carry rivers called
Dulas, gave it distinct advantages as a meeting place. Since it was
also about equidistant from other major towns, Dolgellau and
Aberystwyth, it was a logical place for a market, and in 1291 a
market charter was granted. The allotted day was Wednesday and
even now a street market set up by travelling stall-holders is still
held on that day. It is the association with Owain Glyndwr for which
the town is famous however.

Glyndwr is an enigmatic man in Welsh history, a man of
sophistication and learning, and with dreams of the greatness of
Wales as a culturally separate nation from England, and yet a
butcher of prisoners and ravager of towns. Even as a rebel leader he
appears to have represented a dichotomy, for though he was a
trained soldier and could claim to be a true Welsh leader, he was
also a middle-aged man when the rebellion started.

Glyndwr was born around 1355 to a father who could claim
descent from the princes of North Wales, and a mother who could
claim descent from the Royal line of Deheubarth in South Wales.
Owain's father died young and, as was occasionally the custom
anyway, he was sent as a page to the important family of Fitzalan,
one of the Norman marcher lords. There he became skilled in
fighting, practising long and hard with weapons and also training in
an athletic manner that was unusual for the day. The training
included gymnastics in armour and distance running, which must
have toughened him considerably. He mixed with the nobility of
England and fought for the English king against the French and
Scots. He displayed such bravery and ferocity that he became a
legend and had ballads composed about him 'resplendent in gold

and scarlet trappings of the finest kind', driving the Scots before him like 'a flock of goats' with nothing but the jagged end of his broken lance. When approaching 50, or at least over 40, he retired to his lands at Sycharth, towards Corwen. The peace and tranquillity that the bards found there was not to last, for in 1400 there was dispute over lands between Owain and his marcher lord neighbour, Lord Grey. The situation was clear, Owain was in the right, but Parliament found in Grey's favour declaring, 'what care we for these barefoot Welsh doggies'. Glyndwr was incensed, but before anything further could be done Grey, anxious no doubt to acquire all the Welshman's lands, betrayed him yet again. The King, raising an army for Scotland, summoned Owain to join it, but entrusted the message to Grey, who did not pass it on, making it appear that Owain had refused the royal call.

Glyndwr was a proud man. His physical strength and courage were matched by his appearance: he was tall and wore his hair at shoulder length when the fashion was for close cropping. The blows to his pride were intolerable. With several hundred men Owain sacked Ruthin, Grey's capital, and several smaller towns, but his force was routed by a small English army and scattered. Henry IV marched to Caernarvon, Owain's lands were confiscated and peace restored. Henry breathed a sigh of relief and thought it was all over. He was wrong.

In 1401 the Tudors of Anglesey captured Conwy, a bold action which ended, as we shall see when Conwy is reached, despicably. But however pointless and appalling the act was, as a signal it was remarkable for much of Wales saw it as a gesture of Welsh defiance against the oppression of England. Owain raised a small army and, as we have seen, against all the odds won a decisive victory at Hyddgen. Sensing a dream coming true, more and more men came over to Owain and the rebellion spread. Owain used guerilla tactics which were well suited to the terrain but a large body of his men were caught eventually at Pilleth in the north of old Radnorshire by a large English army. The action was appallingly bloody and ended with the English army fleeing leaving dead and dying by the hundred. From the earliest days Owain had been touched by savagery, the sackings and firing of towns having been ruthlessly carried out. Here, however, the brutality sank to new depths as we read, 'After the batayle ful schamefully the Walsch women cute of mennes membris and pyt hem in here mouthis'. There were no survivors, and the English were required to buy the corpses for burial. It seems that the latent hatred born of years of (effective) slavery was being exorcised in one go. Henry IV was appalled. Owain had requested aid from Scotland and Ireland and, fearful that he might receive it, Henry marched 100,000 men into Wales in late 1402. The terrain and the notorious Welsh weather, together with the guerilla tactics, forced them to retreat. The winter was the worst for years and the bards told that Owain could conjure up this weather for the defeat of his enemies.

Throughout 1403 Owain gained further lands until it was feared he might invade England itself. By 1404 he was so confident and so much in command that he could be openly crowned and then call a parliament here at Machynlleth. He declared his aims as a separate state of Wales which was to have its own archbishop at St. David's appointed by the Pope, a law system and parliaments based on that of Hywel Dda, and universities to promote Welsh learning and culture. Emissaries were sent to continental Europe and to Scotland, and the French prepared an army for the invasion of England. But when at last Owain was in a good position to defeat Henry, he failed. A French fleet landed at Milford Haven in 1405, the last hostile invasion of Britain, and the combined Welsh and French force marched on England. Eight miles from Worcester Owain stopped. There was no battle, no decisive thrust, only indecision and a slow retreat. The French went home and the tide turned against Owain. When Henry appointed his 16-year-old son Prince Henry to the command of the army that would retake Wales the tide ebbed quickly. The castles that the rebels had taken, Harlech, Aberystwyth, were all retaken, some of Owain's best captains were killed or captured and executed and by 1412 without ever having fought a decisive battle Prince Henry had stilled the noise of revolt. By 1415 the country was so quiet that the new king (Henry IV had died in 1413) offered Owain pardon if he would submit. He refused and was never heard of again. The rumour was that he retired to his daughter's house near Kentchurch on the

Parliament House and tourist office, Machynlleth

banks of the Wye. By 1417 it was said that he was dead.

And what of Wales? It can be argued that Glyndwr was no more savage than his warlord contemporaries, that his scorched earth policy was necessary to deny the English provisions, that his looting was necessary to feed his army. But Wales was ravaged, its dreams of nationhood smashed, its people subdued and shackled. The people of Wales could surely be forgiven for seeing in Glyndwr a man who had promised them everything and delivered them only sorrow. Far from that he was, and is, revered, as Joan of Arc was in France, as a supreme patriot. Later, when Tudor kings and queens ruled England and Wales, the magnetism of the man that had led so many so far touched England too. Shakespeare has him thus –

Castlereagh memorial clock, Machynlleth

In faith, he is a worthy gentleman;
Exceedingly well-read, and profited
In strange concealments; valiant as a lion,
And wondrous affable, and as bountiful
As mines of India.

By then, of course, Welsh bowmen had helped the English king to
win at Agincourt.

Glyndwr's coronation and his parliament were held in a building
now occupied by the Parliament House in the main, Maengwyn,
Street. The present building is now believed to have been built later
than 1400, but it is certainly medieval and one of only eight listed
buildings in the old county of Montgomeryshire. Next to the house
is a building of the early twentieth century, though it was

constructed in Tudor style. The two buildings house the tourist office and the Owain Glyndwr Institute, which stages exhibitions during the summer months. To the east of Parliament House, and on the opposite side of Maengwyn Street, is the Court House of the Lords of the Manor that was built, as the inscription notes, by Owen Pugh in 1628. At the other end of Maengwyn Street is the Clock Tower that is such a distinctive feature of the town. The view down the street to the tower from the Court, or Parliament House, is a delight, the wide vista being concentrated by the clock at the street end. The tower was built by the townsfolk themselves to commemorate the coming of age, in 1873, of Viscount Castlereagh, the eldest son of the Marquess of Londonderry who lived at Plas Machynlleth. The tower is 78 feet tall. Plas Machynlleth itself is south of the tower behind an impressive wall and near an equally impressive array of trees and rhododendron bushes. The Plas is dated 1653, though this is the date of the earliest parts, as the present frontage dates from the mid-nineteenth century. The Plas is now offices for business and the town council, but is in need of some restorative work.

Going north from the clock Royal House stands on the corner of Penrallt Street and Garsiwn Lane. This is probably the oldest house in the town as it certainly dates from the fourteenth century and is, therefore, older than Parliament House. At the top of Garsiwn Lane there is a fine row of weaver's cottages from 1820, which are a reminder of the flannel industry that was important to the town for a long period, right through to the latter half of the nineteenth century.

The church of St. Peter pre-dates, in parts, the Royal House by about a century, though it has seen considerable rebuilding and renovation. It is certainly true that there was a priest here in 1201 as in that year 'Kennig of Machenthleith' witnessed an agreement between the Prince of Powys and the abbey of Strata Marcella. The present church is very English in appearance but inside has something of the austerity of a Welsh chapel. Of the nonconformist chapels the Methodist building in Maengwyn Street is a very pleasant example of the type.

Leaving Machynlleth, the wayfarer follows the main road with

The Dyfi bridge north of Machynlleth

great care to the Dyfi bridge. It was at this point that there was the last ford of the river before the sea. That was, of course, a contributory factor to the siting of the town, the distance between town and river being a measure of the seasonal flooding of the Dyfi. There has been a bridge here since 1533 when a London merchant left £6 13s 4d towards its construction in his will. That bridge, a wooden structure, lasted an amazing 150 years. The current bridge was built in 1805, for £250 15s, and is the second stone structure. At this point the Dyfi is still a beautiful sight, wide and placid, but gives little impression of the torrent that carves such a wonderful progress through the land around Mallwyd and Dinas Mawddwy on its way from its birthplace, Craiglyn Dyfi, high in the Aran mountains. All ideas on beauty are subjective, but it is likely that the valleys of the Dyfi and the Mawddach, which will be crossed farther north, would be high on everyone's list.

Cross the bridge and go left on the A493 until a lane goes off right (north) at (741019). Follow this lane as it climbs northward. It is notable for the back views to Machynlleth and the Dyfi and its shadiness, the trees being excellent. At the Y-junction take the left fork. From the gate on the left a few yards up from here the wayfarer has to reach open hill at Foel y Geifr (710050). This can be achieved by following the rights of way clearly marked on O.S. 1:25,000 Outdoor Leisure Map to Snowdonia National Park (Cader Idris/Dovey Forest) as going through the forest. This diligent search starts by going across to the forest. An alternative of going straight on up the path to the forest and basically northward on forest tracks to the hill seems preferable to all concerned. From Foel y Geifr go west and descend to Bryneglwys quarry. The view to Cader Idris beyond the Tal-y-llyn valley from here is quite superb.

Tal-y-llyn

Now the quarry buildings are gone and the mountain is quiet. In its day however the Bryneglwys quarry rivalled Corris, on the other side of Tarren y Gesail. The history of the slate industry is dealt with more fully when the route reaches Blaenau Ffestiniog, to the north, as that town could more accurately claim to be the capital of Welsh slate. Here the slate was of good quality and quarrying began in 1847. A newly formed company, Aberdovey Slate, ran into problems in 1859 when the Corris quarries were connected to the Dovey railway and via it down to a small quay on the river Dyfi at Derwenlas and could therefore easily undercut the price of slate from Bryneglwys. The distance between the two quarries was only 4 miles, but as the journey also included a haul up over the mountain it was impractical. Bryneglwys had therefore to rely on the original method of shifting slates, by packhorse to Aberdyfi. The situation was something that could not be tolerated indefinitely. Either the company built its own access to the sea or it went broke, and so in 1864 the decision was made to build a railway along the valley of the Afon Fathew from Abergynolwyn to Tywyn. The decision to build only as far as Tywyn was taken because by then the standard gauge railway, now the Cambrian Coast line of British Rail, had reached as far as Llwyngwril, north of Tywyn. There was a slight

The lane to Foel y Geifr

hitch in that the connection between Aberdyfi and Machynlleth was
to have been made by bridge across the Dyfi estuary from Aberdyfi
itself to Ynyslas. This ambitious scheme failed and the line north of
the Dyfi was to remain isolated for three years until sense prevailed
and it was linked to Machynlleth via a bridge near what is now Dyfi
Junction a little way north of Glandyfi. The quarry company's
railway was to be narrow gauge, with re-loading on to the main
line's trucks at Tywyn. To connect the quarry to the railway the
immense inclines down the bank of the Nant Gwernol were built. A
continuation of winding engine inclines and tramways then joined
the quarry to the railway terminus. The trucks on the incline were
self-acting, that is the full one going down pulled an empty one back
up, but a brake was still required. If the cable broke, or if the cable
to truck coupling failed, then both wagons fell away towards the
incline base. The result was, obviously, disastrous, and some bits of

wreckage can still be found in the stream by the patient visitor with a taste for the unusual.

The quarry workings themselves were a combination of mining, as at Llechwedd and Oakeley, Blaenau Ffestiniog, and galleried quarry, as at Penrhyn, Bethesda. In this case the difference was in the seaming of the slate. The 'narrow' vein produced a soft slate, but one which could be cleaved into very thin sheets and which was, therefore, very desirable. Unfortunately the seam was very patchy and the first company bankrupted itself in its efforts to excavate a workable mine. The 'broad' vein was of a very hard and long-lasting slate which did not cleave into a thin sheet, producing instead a relatively heavy slate. The broad seams were excellent, but as there were fewer palaces etc. being built than houses they could not, of themselves, make the quarry pay. The first company wound up in 1883. The new company soldiered on but closed the quarry in 1909. The decision was very sudden, overnight Abergynolwyn becoming a town with no jobs for anyone. A new company opened the quarry again in 1911 and it continued to operate, totally against the odds, until 1947 when it closed again, this time for good. Even at that stage the company had not planned to finish. Close attention had been paid to the site by the Mines Inspector for several years and though conditions were bad, there having been no investment since the 1880's and much of the machinery being of that vintage, the quarry always managed to acquire a little grace. Small rockfalls in the mine chambers had become frequent and then, as if Bryneglwys itself was no longer prepared to live on borrowed time, one day the roof fell in just after the men had departed. To stabilise the whole area several other chambers were then dynamited. Great care must be taken at the site. Much of it is on private land, and the casual explorer runs a great risk of injury as man-eating shafts and chasms abound, and much of the old building work is in a precarious state.

Below the quarry is the village of Abergynolwyn, less of a ghost town than the buildings at the quarry site represent as the Forestry Commission now offers local employment. There was a hamlet here, little more than the odd couple of cottages, in the days before the quarry, but the town as we see it is a mid-nineteenth-century development, the three main streets, of 70 houses, having been built

for quarrymen by the earliest company. As with all Welsh villages there are chapels, three here, and a church as well serving a community that seems hardly big enough to support one. The history of the village suggests a more equitable life-style than that followed in the large quarries of North Wales. There was a field that the company rented out, at a farthing per square yard, for allotments. The bakery would bake the villagers' own dough for a penny a loaf, and roast chickens at Christmas. The railway brought in goods from Tywyn, though the village, being above the station level, was served with its own incline. To minimise the inconvenience that this caused the incline was continued as a tramway behind all the houses to give a to-the-door service. The trucks also took away the contents of filled cess-pits, a most welcome service in a community well separated in time from modern sanitation. The effect of the closure of the quarries was, inevitably, catastrophic. This was especially true of the sudden closure in 1909, though the situation was retrieved when the quarry re-opened within two years. Later closures were more gradual allowing the villagers to drift away.

It is for the railway that runs from it to Tywyn rather than the quarries, however, that the village is well known. Strangely it is called the Tal-y-llyn railway, despite never having been to, or ever having been projected to go to, Tal-y-llyn. Most authorities believe that it is likely that the English quarry-owners got the name wrong or, more likely, could not be bothered to get it right! In its original form the railway ran from Tywyn King's, named from the owner of the terminal site, to Nant Gwernol, but the train rapidly became a passenger line as well as a slate carrier, the passengers being ferried between Abergynolwyn and Tywyn Pendre, so that the quarry owners could maintain their own terminals, free of passenger encumbrance. On the modern line King's is called Wharf, which is, effectively, what it originally was as slate was stored and then shipped out on the Cambrian line. The passenger line was opened in 1866 with no intermediate stops, though these followed shortly. At first engines were operated out of Abergynolwyn which suited the driver, a villager, well. When the engine-sheds at Pendre were completed however he was required to take up and leave the engine there. For the journey to Pendre he was given a gravity trolley which he pushed home with one of the trains. At the end of the day he was marooned in Pendre and faced a long, and uphill, journey home. Not surprisingly he soon tired of this and resigned. His replacement was a Tywyn man who excelled himself by driving the train off the end of the line at King's and on to the Cambrian track – a different gauge and at right angles! He was promptly sacked.

The gauge of the railway was 2ft 3in to standardise with the trucks in use on the quarry incline, and the Tal-y-llyn was the first of all the Welsh narrow-gauge lines to run a passenger service and that was built to operate with steam engines from commencement. Because the passenger service terminated at a distance from the Cambrian line the company ran a donkey and cart for passengers connecting with it. Part of the duties of the employees was to cut grass near Pendre station to make hay for the winter feed of the donkey. In the last years of the nineteenth century, and the early years of the twentieth, the growth of tourism allowed the railway to survive the fall in slate trade. One trip that brought in the Victorian traveller was the grand tour by the Corris railway from Machynlleth to Corris, then by horse-drawn carriage down to Tal-y-llyn lake and on to Abergynolwyn to catch the narrow gauge down to the standard gauge for Machynlleth. The train carried the Royal Mail and operated a curious service for the earliest members of the hill-walking fraternity by towing them in a slate wagon to Abergynolwyn and leaving the wagon there for them to ride back to Tywyn, assisted by gravity and helped by a brake fitted to the wagon. What they were not told was that it was *not* downhill all the way and that the uphill sections had to be overcome by pushing. By the thirties pushing had become part of the daily round of passengers as the railway, track and stock, was wearing out. Neither slate nor passengers ever paid well enough for proper investment, and the company rarely had both at once. The line struggled on until 1950 by which time it was the oldest private railway in the world, but then it seemed likely to become another derelict reminder of the area's short-lived industrial past. At that time it was taken over by a group of amateurs who contributed many skills, a quantity of money and, most importantly, enthusiasm and energy in

Tal-y-llyn lake and valley from the north

considerable abundance. Now the railway thrives, and rightly so. It
travels towards one of the finest valleys in the whole of Wales in
Tal-y-llyn, and has a station near the beautiful Dolgoch falls. The
trip from Nant Gwernol to Tywyn takes about an hour in either
direction and seems an excellent way of re-stocking depleted food
supplies or just idling away a rest day with, perhaps, a few hours
relaxation near the sea.

The village lies in the Dysynni valley dominated by Tal-y-llyn
lake at its northern end. The valley is part of a great fault that
continues to Bala, sculpted by later glaciation.

From the bridge over the Dysynni the straightforward route
northward follows the lane north-westward to the cross-roads. Left
from here, about 1½ miles over Pont Ystumanner, is Craig y Aderyn
or Bird Rock, one of the strangest features of the Dysynni valley.
Here four miles inland there is a seabird nesting colony, not of

herring gulls that now appear to nest anywhere, but of about 30 breeding pairs of cormorants. Many, many years ago the sea lapped the foot of Bird Rock and the cormorants are probably a vestigial colony of those far-off days. It is a strange sight to stand below the rock and watch the birds circling high above. The visitor should also note the enormous fertility of the lower, guano-rich slopes.

Our route is to the right, however, passing almost immediately Castell-y-Bere. This was one of the greatest of the Welsh castles, making here a distinction between castles built by the Welsh and those built in Wales by the English. Though lacking the sophistication of English castles (such refinements as the portcullis) it was placed in a very strong position and must have been formidable. It was begun in the early thirteenth century, probably by Llywelyn the Great, and was the royal castle of the Princes of Wales until the conquest of Edward I caused Llywelyn the Last to abandon it. Llywelyn's brother, Dafydd, then occupied the castle and put up a token show of resistance until both the brothers were killed in 1282. The castle was destroyed by Edward, no doubt ridding himself of it because it meant more as a symbol of defiance than it did as a stronghold. Since that time it has decayed away, though the general plan is discernible and much of the basic thirteenth-century work is still visible. The contrast with the Edwardian castles of Harlech and Conwy to the north is profound, the site here being little more than a ruin of old stones. In that sense it is a sad site, as it could be seen as representing the struggle of Wales to gain independence from England.

On again, through Llanfihangel-y-Pennant, we reach a ruined cottage. This was the home of Mary Jones, a girl who saved hard for enough money to buy a Bible in Welsh and when she had the money trekked bare-foot to Bala, a round trip of 50 miles, in order to obtain it from the minister there, Thomas Charles. When she arrived she found that the last one had been sold and that no more would be printed. Charles was so moved by the story that he gave her his own Bible, and the incident is reputed to have prompted him to found the British and Foreign Bible Society. The society still possesses Mary's Bible, but here at the cottage there is only a

Castell-y-Bere with Cader Idris

memorial to the event.

From the cottage our route follows the pony track up the valley of
the Cader stream and then up to the col between Cyfrwy and
Carnedd Lwyd. Take the Cyfrwy ridge, a marvellous edge with
good views to the northern face of Cader Idris and Llyn y Gadair,
up to the high point of Pen y Gadair.

In choosing this route to the summit the wayfarer has passed
some very interesting sites, but he has missed Llyn Cau, arguably
the finest lake in Wales, and the entrance to Cwm Cau, one of the
most dramatic entrances in Wales. To see these the wayfarer must
follow the B4405 past Tal-y-llyn lake to (730113) where a track
leads off north-west. The track starts in wonderful style with a
stream to ford and a deeply wooded path to follow, but soon breaks
out to open hill with the top of Craig Cau lifting above the ridge
ahead. The walker rounds a mound or two and there is Cwm Cau

Cwm Cau and Craig Cau, Cader Idris

with Llyn Cau nestling at the foot of the black cliffs. It is an
enchanted spot. To continue to the summit of Pen y Gadair the
wayfarer goes south of the lake and takes the obvious track over
Craig Cau.

Snowdonia National Park

Cader Idris

Cader Idris is the first of the truly mountainous regions of Wales to be met by the traveller walking north. It is disappointing that so pure a summit should not reach 3,000 feet, and at 2,927 feet Pen y Gadair is lower than Aran Mawddwy and only just higher than the rounded Pen y Fan in the Brecon Beacons. It is said that those who spend a night alone on Cader Idris come down either as madmen or poets, a saying that has now become synonymous with the peak. The aphorism is a general Welsh one, however, and was transferred here fairly recently, having been first applied to Maen d'ur Arddu on Snowdon. Those who do spend the night here can stay comfortable, however, as a substantial, though door-less, hut sits on the top of Pen y Gadair itself. This hut replaces a flimsier one in which an old lady used to set up a tea shop for visitors many years ago!

The name means chair of Idris though who Idris was is a matter of dispute. He could have been one of the legion of Welsh giants, though the only giant to have actually been connected with the mountain was Gwyn ap Nudd who hunted the hills with hounds for the souls of those who had died on the cliffs. Alternatively it could be from Idris ap Gwyddno, a seventh-century Merioneth prince who fought a decisive battle against the Irish in the area. Since that battle is occasionally referred to as the slaughter of the Severn it could have been fought as far away as Plynlimon, which leaves us no closer to the truth.

Any ascent of the mountain is worthwhile but to see the best that Cader Idris can offer in terms of scenery the wayfarer should visit Cwm Cau. This is arguably the finest glacial corrie in Wales, with the steep cliffs of Craig Cau rising above the dark waters of Llyn Cau. The lake, together with Llyn y Gadair to the north, was beautifully described by the bard Gwilym Cowlyd in a Welsh verse known as an englyn. In deference to the language of the original it will be given in Welsh –

Cader Idris from the north-east

> Y llynnau gwyrddion llonydd – a gysgant
> Mewn gwasgod o fynydd;
> A thynn heulwen ysblennydd
> Ar len y dwr lun y dydd.

translated as –

> The calm green lakes are sleeping in the mountain shadow,
> And on the water's canvas bright sunshine paints the picture of
> the day.

The cwm is also of interest to the naturalist, the cliffs supporting an arctic-alpine group of plants as well as a fine group of upland birds, raven and ring ousel.

From the summit of Pen y Gadair traverse Cyfrwy to gain Rhiw

Gwredydd (691135) from where a descent northward can be made. Go west, under the crags of Craig-las, to the road at (678144) where the farm track can be followed with continuation to the northern Cregennen lake. This excellent lake can now be reached by a waymarked track from Arthog that can be reversed, following the western side of the stream down to the main road, the A493, at (646146). An alternative is to reach the same point via a minor road from the lakeside, but this misses an excellent piece of walking, which can be a little crowded in summer since its inclusion in the Barmouth town guide.

From Arthog a footpath leads down to the Mawddach estuary and along to the railway bridge. Beyond the Mawddach estuary and the spit of land that carries Fairbourne there was once, in the days before Arthur, a huge sea wall that held back the sea from the fertile stretch of land of Cantref Gwaelod. Sadly the king of the land, Gwyddno Garanhir, entrusted the maintenance of the wall to men who could not be trusted and it fell into disrepair. Seeing its neglect and a huge storm gathering, Prince Elphin, Gwyddno's son, valiantly warned the people of the hundred villages of Cantref Gwaelod. The people made for high ground and were saved, but the wall was breached and Cantref Gwaelod flooded for ever. Prince Elphin later found a baby washed up on the salmon weir he had built on the Mawddach. The baby grew up to be the great bard Taliesin which gave Elphin some joy in compensation for the loss of his beloved land.

To the left as we cross the Mawddach is the small village of Fairbourne which is the unlikely spot for yet another of the 'great little trains' of Wales. Here a 15-inch-gauge track carries diesel and steam trains along a two-mile track on the sea front. As a ferry crosses the estuary from the track-end to Barmouth it is worth considering the train/boat method of reaching the town. This would be the highly recommended method of reaching Barmouth if it was not for the viaduct which is such an extraordinarily fine method of doing so, perhaps the best town approach on the route, or in Wales as a whole. The viaduct was built to take the railway into the town in 1860, but, as with several other interesting buildings in Barmouth, the construction was not without its problems. A particularly violent

Llyn Cregennen with Cader Idris

storm blew most of the structure away at an advanced state, in the
first attempt to bridge the river. It is worth remembering if you plan
to tramp across it in walking boots with a pack befitting a wayfarer
along the spine of Wales, that doubts are now being cast on the
bridge's safety, wood-boring marine creatures having demolished a
fair proportion of the underwater piling. Actually the pack would
need to be fairly heavy as the doubts have been expressed only
about the continuing usage of the bridge to carry trains. On a lighter
note perhaps the wayfarer could answer an intriguing question, or at
least one that intrigues the author, what did those marine creatures
live on before man evolved to the point where he could build
wooden ships and railway bridges?

From the centre of the bridge the wayfarer is treated to a view of
the Mawddach that vies with the Dyfi for the title of finest river
valley and estuary in Wales. Many have spoken of the incomparable

Llyn Cregennen with Bryn Brith

beauty of the Mawddach estuary, one, Rhys Davies, making an
acidic judgement on the town at the same time declaring that the
estuary was 'displaying what He can create – in comparison with the
work of man in Barmouth'. The description of the estuary is,
perhaps, the only truly accurate one that can be offered, and even
that does not offer any hope of capturing the essence of its beauty,
the play of colours, light on water. Nothing can. The judgement on
the town is harsh. In one sense it has truth in that Barmouth is both
seaside town and venerable Welsh port and suffers from the
duplicity, but it is the old port that disclaims the comparison. It may
not have the essential beauty of the Mawddach, but it does have a
distinct character.

Barmouth

The two-edged nature of the town, mentioned above, extends even

Barmouth from the Mawddach bridge

to its name. The true name is Abermaw, itself a diminutive form of
Abermawddach, but years of usage allowed a vernacular form
Bermo to evolve and this was promptly Anglicised to Barmouth. As
a town its history is very short. It was mentioned in the
Merionethshire survey of 1565 instituted by the advisors of
Elizabeth I concerned at the incidence of piracy in the Irish/Celtic
sea. Then it was 'Abermowe, beinge likewise a haven havinge no
habitacion. But only foure howses'. The punctuation is not good but
it is clear that as recently as 400 years ago the town was an
undistinguished place. With the expansion of trading on a
countrywide basis that was evolving, Barmouth was bound to
increase in importance, coastal waters being a safe place for trading
boats that could carry relatively large cargoes quickly. Barmouth's
trade and importance, as seen by the number of ships belonging to
the port, increased steadily, despite receiving a setback during the

Afon Mawddach from the bridge

Civil War when what then constituted the town was looted and
sacked by a detachment of Parliamentarian soldiers. By the end of
the eighteenth century Barmouth was established as the primary
port of Merionethshire, winning out over Aberdyfi because of the
ship-building and repair industries which had sprung up close to the
port and along the Mawddach towards Dolgellau.

Much of Barmouth's trade was in coarse woollen cloth produced
in Merionethshire. Ironically, the cloth was mainly exported to the
American colonies where it was used to clothe slaves working on
cotton plantations whose product had, itself, killed off large sections
of the British woollen industry. Thus deprived and exploited Welsh
workers clothed even more deprived and exploited black slaves who
helped their masters impoverish English weavers. The American
War of Independence ended the trade at a stroke and the limited
European market was destroyed equally quickly by war with France

in the 1790's. Nevertheless the town improved its harbour in 1797 hoping to take advantage of slate, the newest Welsh industry. Because it was not near to one of the quarry sites Barmouth could not benefit directly, but many of its ships moved slates from Porthmadog and Port Dinorwic, and the shipbuilding yards were active building slate traders. Unfortunately however the age of the train arrived and with it the decline of the shipbuilding industry, and of the town as a port. Today there are fishermen here, mainly catching lobsters, but in the main the boats are pleasure craft.

Luckily for the town the decline in the port traffic occurred at the same time as the increase in enthusiasm for sea-bathing and seaside holidays. Both of these are relatively recent innovations, despite the idea that the great British holiday has been with us since time immemorial. Royal approval of sea bathing provided the impetus and Barmouth was equipped with bathing machines by the start of the nineteenth century. These impressive devices were for the use of women so that they should not be seen bathing. Elsewhere they were horse-drawn or winched into and out of the sea. Here they were, initially, fixed so that the bather was marooned for considerable periods by the tide. With the bathers, especially after the coming of the railway when they could arrive in far greater numbers, came a boom in building with inns, hotels and shops. For the Victorians Barmouth was a delight, the list of notables of the time who came being long, and including Charles Darwin as well as the more romantic names that we usually associate with such spots, Tennyson, Wordsworth and Shelley.

It was to the old town that the romantics were drawn, and it is this area that should be visited to feel the character of the old port, and see the great contrast to the seaside resort below. Below is correct, for the old port is hewn out of a series of rocky steps with alleyways and passages that connect together in a beautiful, haphazard way. Here the old port is seen to perfection, the houses jutting out of the cliff itself, often reached by stone bridges because of the angles. Here lived a Mrs Talbot who helped Barmouth to a place in history by her friendship with John Ruskin the social reformer. Impressed by his ideas on housing and social welfare, she gave him some old cottages on the Rock to set up a small housing experiment. Ruskin

Rhinog Fawr
(720 m
2362')
2250'
2000'
1750'
1500'
1250'
Bwlch Drws Ardud
1250'
1500'
1750'
2000'
Rhino
Fach
(711m
233
2250'
Llyn
Hywel
2000'
2250'
Y Llethr
(754 m
2473')
Crib-y-rhiw
2000'
2250'
Maes y Garnedd
Cwm Nantcol
Moel-y-
blithcwm
A 496
Harlech
Moelfre
Llyn
Bodlyn
Diffwys
(750 m
2460')
Dyffryn
Ardudwy
Pont
Scethin
2000'
310
RHINOGS
Gors-y-Gedol
Cromlech
Llyn
Irddyn
Tal-y-bont
Llawllech
Carneddau
Hengwm
(588 m
1930')
1750'
1500'
Bwlch y Rhiwgyr
1250'
1000'
305
A 496
Dolgellau
WT
station
Cardigan
Bay
Garn
(265m
869')
750'
750'
500'
250'
Barmouth
Afon Mawddach

called his community the Guild of St. George and it flourished, the
tenants paying a fixed rent and thriving on self-help. The latter was
less influenced by Ruskin than by a Frenchman, Auguste Guyard, a
friend of Alexander Dumas and Victor Hugo, and a believer in
self-sufficiency, an idea that many believe to have been invented
only very recently. Guyard sought refuge here when France went to
war with Germany and became a great friend of Ruskin, believing
in his social theories and, on a more practical note, helping tenants
to grow vegetables by terracing the land. When he died he was
buried on the hillside above his cottage. It is not for this attempt to
create the perfect society that Mrs. Talbot and Barmouth have
achieved fame, but for the creation of the National Trust. In 1895
Mrs. Talbot helped create the Trust, probably again with Ruskin's
ideas in mind, by giving land on Dinas Oleu, the fortress of light, the
first such donation. A plaque notes the gift, and that it is 'to be kept
and guarded for the enjoyment of Barmouth for ever'. The initial
idea of the Trust was to preserve Britain's coast-line and, therefore,
coastal scenery. Mrs. Talbot died in 1917 at the great age of 93. If
she were alive today she would have been very proud, and with
good reason, of the work of the National Trust today. Below her
house, Ty'n-y-ffynon, is a fine memorial inscription in the rock, less
to her than to the ideas of the Trust, and composed by another
co-founder of it, Canon H.D. Rawnsley.

St. John's church over near the Peak as Craig y Gigfron is called
locally, though modern, the foundation stone being laid by Princess
Beatrice in 1889, has been claimed to be among the best in North
Wales. The church is another of the structures that had construction
problems. The tower collapsed without warning when construction
was almost complete, severely damaging the main body of the
church. Above St. John's on the Peak is another collection of
intricate alleyways and pleasant cottages. One group is called Spion
Kop, not after Anfield in deference to Liverpudlian
holiday-makers, but after the Boer War battle hill from which the
football crowd terracing also gets its name.

Elsewhere there are other interesting buildings including several
old inns, but interest of a different kind can be found in the R.N.L.I.
maritime museum at the harbour, near where the current Barmouth

Rhinog Fach and Rhinog Fawr with, between them, Bwlch Drws Ardudwy, from the east

lifeboat is housed. The museum was set up to help finance the
service for although entrance is free there is a donation box. Inside
the small building there are models of the various types of lifeboats,
as well as mementoes from the history of the service in Barmouth,
which stretches back to 1828. It is an interesting collection, and a
fitting tribute to a group of brave volunteers. Above the harbour the
herring gulls wheel continuously. This gull is now very abundant
due to its habit of feeding on inland rubbish tips, for which it is
much maligned. Despite this its call still seems to epitomise the
seaside and on hearing it thoughts turn to hot days on long sandy
beaches. Barmouth has those as well, but the sea-bather should
beware, for the town is reputed to have a sea-monster living just off
shore which has been seen for about 100 years or so, with the best
sighting as recently as 1975 when it was spotted by six schoolgirls.

When leaving Barmouth the wayfarer is spoilt for choice with regard to paths as there are several that leave the old and steep section of the town. As good as any is the signed path between the houses that stand a little to the west of the end of the Mawddach bridge. This path leads east of Garn (618165) to a road at (622166) and on towards the WT station (625175), and Bwlch y Rhiwgyr (627200). At that point there is a problem. The clear way forward now is to traverse Llawlech to Diffwys (661234) and on to Y Llethr (661258). From Y Llethr northward are the Rhinogs. The Rhinogs are the only piece of Cambrian rock traversed by a route that was to have been designated the Cambrian Way. This lump of Cambrian strata sits over the synclinal Ordovician strata that form Snowdon to the north and Cader Idris to the south. This geological position gives the range its alternative name of the Harlech Dome, the castle town being set at the western foot of the range. This is Wales at its wildest. It draws you in on the whaleback of Diffwys, gives you a glimpse at Y Llethr, winds itself up on the two Rhinog peaks and then unleashes the wilderness to the north. The Rhinogs are a superb range, offering uncompromising walking but in exchange glimpses of wild, beautiful country. This country starts at Y Llethr with its view of Llyn Hywel and the steep slabs that slide into it. There is Rhinog Fawr with its curious banded rock strata and then the jumble of rock and vegetation that comprises the north of the range.

Between the Rhinog peaks, Fawr and Fach, the big and small gateposts, is Bwlch Drws Ardudwy, the pass of the gate of Ardudwy. The land of Ardudwy, sandwiched between the peaks and the sea, holds many surprises, not least the legend of the men of Ardudwy, a band of outlaws who rode through the gateway to loot the outside world, returning to their safe lair. They met their end near Llan Ffestiniog according to a weird story that will be related later. However, the walker would not necessarily explore the land of Ardudwy in preference to the wild Rhinogs and that is where the problem referred to above lies. There is no right of way from Llawlech northward along the Rhinog ridge and over the wasteland to Moel Ysgyfarnogod (659347). North-east of that peak a footpath does run up on to the waste land, finishing at (671360), and this path is signed at its access to the minor road at (684359). Several

Pont Scethin

pathways do however traverse the range east-west, one through Bwlch Drws Ardudwy between the Rhinog peaks, one through Bwlch Tyddiad north of Rhinog Fawr and one through Bwlch Gwylin to the south and east of Clip. To the south of the first named pathway there is clear indication of a pathway through Bwlch y Rhiwgyr, but the 'Harlech' sheet of the O.S. Snowdonia Leisure map shows a 350-metre gap in the right of way. Similarly, the pathway at the northern end of the range mentioned above has a similar gap before continuing westward. In both cases the right of way is almost certainly continuous, the missing sections being as a result of problems at parish boundaries, or plain oversight. The existence of these pathways does mean that the wayfarer can reach Llyn Trawsfynydd from Barmouth and see the Rhinogs, but his route is extended into the land of Ardudwy.

In the land of Ardudwy there are the Carneddau Hengwm, which have been called the finest monuments in England and Wales, and

Gors-y-Gedol and Dyffryn Ardudwy cromlechs, also some of the finest in Wales. These lie west of Pont Scethin (634235) one of the most romantic sites in Wales. Pont Scethin lies on a right-of-way traverse of the range, the route following the old coaching road from Bwlch y Rhiwgyr to the bridge. Near the bridge you will pass a memorial stone to Janet Haigh raised by her son. It is a modest, yet striking, tablet and its final phrase 'Courage Traveller' is in keeping with the track's ancient usage and the modern wayfarer facing the Rhinogs.

Pont Scethin still carries a route, a green path, but its sudden appearance, a bridge in the middle of nowhere, can startle. North-west are the ruins of an old coaching inn, another tangible, but less enduring, reminder of a coach ex-Harlech, bound for London, hoping to beat the bandits to the Mawddach. And before the coach there were the drovers.

The route leads north to Cwm Nantcol, the first of two fine cwms on the western flank of the Rhinogs. At the head of Cwm Nantcol is Maes y Garnedd, once the home of Col. John Jones, one of the signatories of Charles I's death warrant. He was hated by the locals who, presumably, were not too sympathetic when Charles II sentenced him to death after the restoration. Samuel Pepys noted one day in his diary that after hanging, drawing and quartering the 'steaming remains' of Jones were towed around London – suggesting that Jones was no more popular in London. Farther down Cwm Nantcol is Salem chapel where Curnow Vosper painted his famous picture of the Welsh at prayer. Locals were paid 6d per sitting in 1910, the painting being 'live', and Shani Owen stood as the central figure. In the folds of her shawl many people see the Devil's head and it is not known whether Vosper intended this as a comment on what he saw as the hypocrisy of people like Shani Owen, or whether it was an accident.

As the eye is drawn to the twin Rhinogs it cannot fail to see the walls, miles and miles of neat walls that climb the steep slopes relentlessly. Here in Nantcol wall building is not merely functional, but an art form.

A path leads north from Maes y Garnedd to Llyn Gloyw and on into Cwm Bychan, the second of the two fine cwms. Cwm Bychan is

Rhinog Fach and Llyn Hywel from Y Llethr

famed not only for its unquestioned rugged beauty, a surprising
contrast to the harsh beauty of the northern Rhinogs, but for the
'Roman' steps that rise up Bwlch Tyddiad beyond Llyn Bychan at
its head. The site is almost certainly not Roman, the spacing of the
steps suggesting a packhorse route.

From Cwm Bychan the wayfarer has the choice of continuing
eastward for Bwlch Gwylin (658329) and on to Trawsfynydd, or of
going westward towards Llyn Fedw (626330) and taking the path to
Trawsfynydd that runs north of the lake. The latter route has little
to recommend it unless the opportunity to visit Harlech castle is
taken.

Whether the wayfarer visits Harlech, or even the land of
Ardudwy, he arrives on the north-east flank of Moel Ysgyfarnogod
and follows the poorly defined path to the minor road beside Llyn
Trawsfynydd. At the road go right and follow it to the footbridge

(702349). Across the lake at every point of this walk can be seen
the Trawsfynydd power station. The generating station is
nuclear-powered, the only British nuclear station built on an inland
site. The reactor buildings were designed by Sir Basil Spence with
Dame Sylvia Crowe as landscape architect. It is a matter of personal
opinion whether they were successful in blending the site in with the
surroundings. The nuclear reactors are of the first generation
'Magnox' type with natural uranium fuel in a magnesium alloy can.

Cross the bridge and take the road through the grey, slate village
to the A470 where, at (708361), a signed pathway leads out on to
hillside again. The wayfarer now heads northward using the masts
of the radio station at (709391) as a beacon when he can. To the
west, 800 metres short of the masts, is Tomen-y-Mur. Here stood a
Roman fort which, despite the fine views, must have been the last
place any Roman soldier wanted to be posted – the very frontier of
the Empire, with pouring rain and pagan savages for company.
Interestingly the fort had a small amphitheatre, or possibly a
cock-pit, the authorities realising, perhaps, that the lot of the soldier
here was not, of itself, a happy one. The fort never saw great service
and was abandoned after a comparatively short time. The Normans
used the existing fortifications and added a motte, but it was never a
popular site and they abandoned it in their turn. Now no stone
remains, only the imprint of banks and mounds.

The site is also the legendary home of Blodeuwedd, the flower
maiden, made by the gods Math and Gwydion for Lleu, nephew of
Gwydion, who had been cursed that he should never have a mortal
wife. Blodeuwedd was made out of the flowers and blossoms of oak,
broom and meadowsweet, for constancy, beauty and gentleness.
But Blodeuwedd while beautiful was neither gentle nor constant,
and fell in love with another. She and her lover decided to kill Lleu,
no straightforward matter as he could not be killed inside or outside
a house, on horseback or on foot. They overcame the problems by
killing him with a poisoned spear as he swam in the nearby Cynfal
stream. At the moment of death he became an eagle which flew
away to the gods to be healed. Restored to health he came back to
Tomen-y-Mur to kill Blodeuwedd's lover. She escaped and fled with
her hand-maidens, but they were so afraid at being pursued that

they walked backwards and all perished when they fell into the Lake of the Maidens at Llan Ffestiniog. Blodeuwedd alone survived and was turned into an owl so that her face would never be seen by day again. This also explains why other birds mob the owl. As we shall see later, however, the lake's name has another derivation.

Our route goes west of the radio station to Sychnant Farm, along the west edge of the wood and down to the A470 (705404). Immediately opposite a path goes down to Cynfal Fawr. This is a small manor house with a seventeenth-century front but later windows. The core of the house is earlier and includes two cruck beams. It was the home of Huw Llwyd, a sixteenth-century soldier (?) but also a bard. Returning from a long campaign in the Low Countries he was not recognised at his home. Thomas Love Peacock records the return this way –

Art thou a Welshman, old soldier, she cried,
Many years have I wandered, the stranger replied,
Twixt Danube and Thames many rivers there be
But the bright waves of Cynfal are fairest to me.

The stone plaque on the house commemorates Huw's grandson Morgan, Puritan writer and mystic who wrote *The Three Birds*, a conversation between Cromwell, a Puritan and an Episcopalian in the characters of Eagle, Dove and Raven.

The wayfarer has the chance to assess the bright waves of Cynfal as the path drops down to the stream and waterfall, before climbing again to emerge in Llan Ffestiniog. This is the original village, the slate industry creating the newer and bigger Blaenau a mile or so farther north. To the east is Llyn Morynion where Blodeuwedd's maidens from Tomen-y-Mur may have drowned. Alternatively the lake could be named after maidens from Clwyd. These were captured by the Ardudwy robbers who were returning to the Rhinogs when they were overtaken by the kinsmen of the maidens and killed. The maidens, who had fallen in love with the Ardudwy men, could not bear the thought of a return to Clwyd and so committed mass suicide in the lake.

Llan Ffestiniog is also the home of Rhys Goch, Red Rhys of

Trawsfynydd power station

Snowdon, a famed bard at the time of Owain Glyndwr, who was a
great ally of the prince and composed war verses noted for their
ferocity. He survived the revolt and lived here to a great age,
perhaps even one hundred years.

To continue take the lane next to the *Pengwern Arms*. At its top
go north-west to the cottage at (697424). Go north again and then
follow the path around westward and on to the A496 (691422).
Turn right (north) and after 150 metres go left to a drive and then a
path going westward. The Afon Goedol is crossed by footbridge
(689424). Here the wayfarer is in the Coed Cymerau Nature
Reserve, an excellent piece of woodland enhanced by the stream.
The route heads west along a path through the wood and emerges
on the hillside to meet the track of the Festiniog railway. Even to
the non-enthusiast this railway is a highlight of the journey.

Festiniog Railway

The history of the railway is linked inextricably with the history of slate in the Blaenau area for, like the Tal-y-llyn to the south, it was constructed as a slate railway. One of the truly remarkable things about the railway is that it linked two places that a decade earlier had not existed. At Blaenau there was only a mountain, at Porthmadog there was only sea. The existence of Porthmadog is the result of the work of one man, William Madocks. He had inherited a fortune from his father and as MP for Boston in Lincolnshire obtained an Act of Parliament to grant him any land reclaimed in the area at the mouth of the Glaslyn river. Madocks had constructed the mile-long causeway, now known as the Cob, connecting the new town and port of Porthmadog to Penrhyn Isaf. His workers were housed in Boston Lodge named after his constituency, and now the engineering works of the Festiniog railway. Behind the port Madocks also constructed a model town at Tremadog. The Glaslyn now empties through sluice gates in the Cob, the tide being held back by the same gates. It is a little sad that in the last few years the names of both town and port have been altered to suggest a name based on Madog, the legendary Welsh discoverer of America, rather than Madocks. This seems to be based on the general feeling that this Englishman should not be commemorated in the heart of Welsh Wales. In fact William Madocks was born in Llandwrnod, Denbighshire. Though Madocks had only intended to reclaim land he was quick to note the potential benefit of the deep-water channel that the Glaslyn carved to the sea beyond the sluice gates. At the time slates from the Blaenau quarries were horse-packed, or carted, to quays near Maentwog on the Afon Dwyryd, a dangerous, tidal river. In 1821 Madocks built the harbour of Porthmadog itself and following his death in 1828 an Act was passed allowing the construction of a railway from the port to Blaenau. The railway was completed in 1836, with a gauge variously reported as 1 ft $10\frac{3}{4}$ in or 1 ft $11\frac{1}{2}$ in. At that time it was for the most part gravity powered, trainloads of trucks falling from Blaenau to Porthmadog complete with a brakeman to prevent disasters and several horse-boxes to haul the empty trucks back along the $13\frac{1}{2}$-mile route. The opening

The Festiniog Railway at Blaenau Ffestiniog

of a tunnel through the Moelwyns in 1842 meant a completely
gravity powered system. At Blaenau the railway was fed by inclines
from the quarries. Since the London and North Western and the
Great Western Railway companies also had lines to Blaenau at later
stages, and all had different stations, the town is of enormous
interest to the railway historian. It is the Festiniog that the tourist
comes to see in general, and the first thing he notices is that the
name is spelt incorrectly. The Anglicised spelling has always been
used, from the first Act, and has now become part of the charm of
the little line. The early history of the railway, indeed of all the
railways, was punctuated with squabbles between themselves and
with the quarry owners. It appears that the owners were a shrewd
lot who had hacked their way upwards and had learnt how to exploit
differences and concerns. The biter did occasionally receive a flesh
wound however. In 1852 J.W. Greaves, the owner of Llechwedd,

wrote bitterly to James Spooner, the local supplier of gunpowder, about Spooner's decision to increase the price of powder. 'I think you should have informed me you had raised the price,' he states and then – 'When Mr. Curtis was here lately I promised to try his powder.' Greaves enclosed a cheque based on the old price of £40 per ton as opposed to the new one of £42. The plea was ignored, the bluff called and Spooner replied that not only was £40 not enough, but that £42 was now £44, and, more to the point, pay up or else no more powder!

This James Spooner was the son of James Spooner, the first engineer of the railway, and another son, Charles, took over the railway when James senior died in 1856. Charles Spooner's first task was to prepare the track for steam locomotives, a dream of his father's during his last years. It was not only the fulfilment of a dream, however, but business necessity, the horse-drawn system being unable to keep up with the increased tonnages of slate. The problem was that existing designs of narrow-gauge engines would not run on the track as it was too narrow and too twisty. The solution was a low, square engine of only 5 tons, the first two being delivered in 1863. Very soon after their arrival the railway opened a passenger service, a description of which offers a beautiful insight into the effect on the neighbourhood of the steam engine – horses galloped, a cow ran over a sow causing much amusement, and the 'amazed specimens of Young Wales' at Blaenau ran from the whistle not knowing whether to laugh or scream.

The passenger traffic was very important to the railway, particularly when the slate trade declined. To ensure a high standard the employees were issued with an 86-page volume of regulations including a very long list of fines for misconduct. This included a 1s fine for being on duty improperly dressed, i.e. without part of the uniform, or 6d for being untidy. Charles Spooner was a hard, though fair, man. It is reported that on one occasion when a signalman made a mistake Spooner trekked down to the signal box, hauled the man out and thrashed him with his walking stick. It was not only the employees who had to conform, passengers were requested 'not to lean over, or put their Feet outside the Carriage, or on the Cushions, nor to throw out Empty Bottles'.

The decline of the slate trade had an adverse effect on the railway's ability to keep up the required level of investment. In the First World War the whole network was taken over as part of a munitions scheme, shells being made at the Boston Lodge works, and this also caused a general decline in the condition of the rolling stock. Between the wars a more general decay set in as economy drives were ordered, winter passenger services were stopped and everything came to a halt in 1939. Following the Second World War the line fell into complete disrepair. Boston Lodge, the engines and stations were vandalised and looted, grass and trees grew over the abandoned track. Finally, as at Tal-y-llyn, rescue came in the form of an enthusiastic preservation society in 1954. Sadly this was too late to prevent a major disruption of the line, the dismantling and then flooding of the line around Tan-y-grisiau by the lower reservoir of the C.E.G.B.'s pumped storage power station. The new society went forward on two fronts, to re-open the line from Porthmadog to Ddualt, a halt in the middle of one of the most beautiful of nowheres, and litigation with the CEGB over compensation on the flooded section. The first was a major success, but the second turned into a long and occasionally bitter campaign ending with the society obtaining substantial, but by then inadequate, compensation for the last section. Only very recently has the section from Dduault to Blaenau been re-opened. That it exists at all is a monument to the amazing energy and tenacity of a remarkable group of railway enthusiasts.

Our route follows the eastern bank of the Tan-y-Grisiau reservoir, keeping the railway in sight but also offering another view of a power station across a lake. This station is of novel design not being a straightforward hydro-electric station, but a pump-storage station. The major problem with electricity is the inability of the generators or users to store it. Batteries work reasonably well with chemical storage of low voltage direct current supplies, but no successful system exists for storing high voltage a.c. supplies. In a system with many small generating units this is not a problem as if more power is needed an extra unit is fired up. With the advent of nuclear power plant, which cannot vary load quickly but is efficient in generating continuous high loads, there was a requirement to store output. Here during quiet hours, usually at night, 'surplus' electricity is used to pump water from the lower reservoir to the upper lake behind the Stwlan dam. Then during periods of high load the water flow is reversed, power being generated as in a normal hydro-electric plant. The power turbine doubles as a water pump. The same principle applies at the bigger station (Dinorwic) in the Llanberis pass.

When the pathway emerges on to the B4414 go left towards Blaenau Ffestiniog. At this point, if indeed not well before, the wayfarer is aware of the slate quarries behind and above the town.

Slate

The splitting quality of some Welsh rocks and their use in building was known very early. Indeed there is evidence that the Romans knew of the usefulness of slate, the fort of Segontium outside Caernarfon having been floored, and perhaps roofed, with Cambrian slate. Since the slate must have been brought at least 5 miles to the site it is inconceivable that the builders used it in preference to locally available rocks for any reason other than its usefulness. Following that usage, that is up to the second century AD, there is an absence of evidence of slate usage until we hear that Edward I stayed in a house in the Nantlle valley that was roofed in slate. While it is unlikely that these slates were as thin, or as neat, as those of today it is clear that the locals had learnt to cleave the rock. Later, when Conwy castle was constructed, the main hall was given a slated roof by Henry le Sclatiere. Despite this and other works involving the slating of roofs, slate was not in general use before the eighteenth century, when the major quarries that characterise the Snowdonia National Park were worked in earnest. During the earliest usage of the tiles the word 'sclatte' was used as description, the word being derived, it is believed, from the French verb 'esclater', to break into pieces, the splitting of the rock into thin sheets being its most characteristic quality. Such rock was, in Welsh, known by two words, either 'llech' for the rock prior to splitting, or 'sglatys' or 'ysglatys' for the particular form of the tile after splitting. By the time the industry started in earnest, however, the Welsh form sclatte had been dropped in favour of slat or slate.

Moelwyn Bach, above Blaenau Ffestiniog

Slate beds are produced by compressive forces during earth
movements. Because of the localised nature of the compressions the
beds were themselves localised. There were five main areas –
around Elidir Fawr at the northern end of the Glyders range where
the Cambrian beds were exploited in the Dinorwic quarries at
Llanberis and the Penrhyn quarries at Bethesda; the Ordovician
beds around Blaenau Ffestiniog; the Ordovician and Silurian beds
around Corris to the north of Machynlleth; the Silurian beds
between Corwen and Llangollen; and the Ordovician beds at
Preseli in old Pembrokeshire. In addition to differences in the age of
the rock comprising the slate bed there is also a considerable
variation in colour, although it is sometimes necessary to see two
slates of differing colour to be able to distinguish between them
accurately. Colour differences also occur within a quarry, the
Dinorwic rock having green, red and blue veins, each further

subdivided by the colour texture or line pattern, so that there could
be a silky, mottled, striped, spotted, curly or hard colour vein. Other
areas were similar, though the Ffestiniog slates are almost
exclusively a solid blue-grey colour.

The first development of the slate on a highly commercial basis
was at the Penrhyn quarry near Bethesda. The site was owned by
Richard Pennant, from the same family as the naturalist Thomas
Pennant, who became the first Lord Penrhyn. The Penrhyn family
built the huge and luxurious Penrhyn Castle to the east of Bangor.
The luxury of the family's lifestyle, and that of the Assheton Smiths,
owners of the Dinorwic quarry, at Vaynol Hall, contrasted fiercely
with the conditions in which the quarrymen lived and raised their
families and it was said by the latter that if you stole a sheep from
the mountain you were hanged, but that if you stole the mountain
itself they made you a lord.

Development of the slate at Ffestiniog followed a little behind the
workings at Dinorwic and Penrhyn, slate at first being worked only
by locals for their own use. This was chiefly because of the difficulty
of removing slates from the town. There was a small quay on the
Afon Dwyryd to the west of Maentwrog, but the journey from the
quarries to the quay was 'both tedious and expensive, (the
quarrymen) not being, as yet, possessed of a railway, they employ
for this purpose about thirty carts, which certainly do not improve
this public road'. The latter was almost certainly the case, the
narrow-wheeled carts heavily laden with slates churning the roads
to such an extent that at one time the Dinorwic quarry owners were
forced to use only broad-wheeled carts. The slates to be found at
Ffestiniog were of superb quality, but in addition to the transport
problems there was also a working problem, the beds being at an
awkward angle and hidden between bands of useless, but hard,
rock. The normal open-cast quarrying was therefore at a
disadvantage because of the need to remove huge quantities of
'rubbish', as it was actually called, before the slate could be reached.
To overcome the problem the Blaenau slate was mined. Even then
it was hard, dangerous work. By the early 1900's the annual death
rate was 3–4 per 100 with an injury rate of 10 per cent in the
quarries and 6 per cent in the mines. One problem was that there

was little first aid or rescue service available at the sites and injured men were invariably manhandled, which made their injuries worse. Crippled and maimed men were a common sight in the slate towns. Some of the accidents were caused by the unskilled use of gunpowder. This was preferred to any other explosive as it caused a 'gentle' bang, that is the pressures during the blast were small and did not shatter the rock unnecessarily. The powder was loaded into the charge hole which, at first, was laboriously drilled by hand, the $7\frac{1}{2}$-foot hole taking 10 hours to drill. The powder was poured in and then tamped down. This itself was an occupation fraught with danger because the tamp rod, or stamper, a rod 30 inches long, $2\frac{1}{2}$ inches in diameter, occasionally fired the powder and turned into a projectile which could, and did, kill the operators. It did offer high entertainment though. In 1902 the Prince and Princess of Wales witnessed a bang at Dinorwic when 2 tons of powder shifted an estimated 100,000 tons of rock.

After the slate had been removed from the face it was taken to the mill for dressing. The actual splitting has always been done by hand, no machine ever having been invented that could split better than a man. The man sat with the slab of rock leaning against his leg and split it with a broad-bladed chisel and a mallet. In general the slates were split at 6–10 to the inch though in the 1862 London Exhibition the Llechwedd quarries exhibited slates at 16 to the inch, and in 1872 another Llechwedd man split at 18 to the inch. Today, to prove that the craft is not dying everywhere, some splitters can achieve 36 to the inch, though not a roof tile size. After splitting the tile was trimmed to size. Initially this was also a hand operation, the man marking the slate with a wooden stick with a nail in it and then giving it a single blow with an iron blade. Trimming machines did achieve some success later. The slates were of standard sizes from ladies through countesses to duchesses, exotic names that seemed preferable to 8×16 or 14×24.

The early working method was for a group of men to buy from the management a square yardage of rock face which they would then work to tiles and sell these back to the management. The buy was for a week or sometimes longer and the agreed price was the 'bargain' and was strictly kept. The men bought gunpowder, fuses and, in the Blaenau mines, candles, and hired tools from the owners and if their bargain was a patch of bad rock then they could work all week and finish up with a loss. It was claimed, by the owners, that the men had to be paid this way, they could not be paid a wage or 'they will do nothing by the day'. Later 'poundage' was introduced to improve matters, this being a guaranteed minimum sum for working so that bad rock bargains did not mean financial losses. A wage system followed, though this was in many instances even worse for the men, as the time period the owners had to wait for payment for delivered slate was passed on to the men directly, so they might go for months without money. In addition during protracted pay negotiations the owners often refused to pay the going rate, paying instead subsist money that was intended to pressurise the men into an early, and low, settlement. The owners also ran what was sometimes, in these remote areas, the only shop and even, on occasions, paid the workers in tickets that could be exchanged only in the company shop. The poverty in some areas was grim. In 1822 the men of the Nanttle quarry asked for a reduction in the price of gunpowder to that paid at other quarries, as they could no longer obtain credit at the local shop, and had not been paid for 21 weeks. Matters could hardly continue in this fashion, and in the last quarter of the nineteenth century the men began to rebel against conditions. The first union was formed at the Glynrhonwy quarry, on Llyn Padern, in early 1874 and the owners closed the quarry. At that time the slate trade was excellent; the owners could afford the strike less than the men who could afford to wait or move elsewhere. Within a month the lock-out was at an end and the union established. At Dinorwic itself the lesson was learned quickly, and within four weeks it too was locked out. Again, this time after five weeks, the owners conceded. In July it was Lord Penrhyn's turn to lock up his quarry. In a bitter exchange of letters between the men's organisers and Penrhyn himself the men pointed out that they were loyal, one of their number having worked in the quarry for more than 60 years, but required a living wage. Penrhyn replied that he could not raise wages for three good reasons. First if he did the quarry would not then give him the profit he required; secondly the men were extremely ungrateful in not realising how generous he was already; and thirdly if he did give them more money they would only bring ruin on their families – presumably because they could not handle the cash properly and would get drunk. Not surprisingly the men were very bitter at this and refused to return until Penrhyn accepted the union and increased their wage. After six weeks he capitulated. While Penrhyn's attitude was clearly patronising it is worth remembering that the quarrymen were a hard-drinking and uncompromising breed, a well-known saying being 'I've had a drop too much and its gone to the wife's head'.

Despite the rise of unionism conditions were still awful by present standards, particularly in the mines of Blaenau Ffestiniog. There the workers lived in houses that were damp with poor drainage and water supplies. Typhoid was endemic and the general overcrowding, together with the high rainfall and inadequate heating, caused a high incidence of TB and pneumonia. The men went to the mine in the rain, worked all day in wet clothes, in wet conditions and with no facilities, and walked home in the rain again. The owners, when challenged by the unions over the conditions, claimed that the men were at fault, as they 'drank too much stewed tea and did not change their underclothes often enough'. This attitude was mirrored in the 1920's when Ellis Davies, the MP for Caernarvon, was fighting for silicosis to be classed as an industrial injury and the Penrhyn quarry doctor maintained that far from being a hazard slate dust was beneficial.

At Blaenau Ffestiniog the slate was mined at the Oakeley quarries, owned by W.G. Oakeley, and at Llechwedd, owned by the Greaves family. Some idea of the effect on the local area can be envisaged from the fact that in 1788 the quarries exported 500 tons of slate, while in 1831 they exported 12,000 tons, a 2,400 per cent rise. In the same period the northern quarries increased by only 450 per cent. The population meanwhile rose from under 700 to several thousand. It was 11,000 by 1900, but had fallen to around 6,000 sixty years later. The industry was always a fluctuating one, but by 1900 the trade was in final decline. Llechwedd cut the week to four days in 1905 and then cut wages by 10–15 per cent in 1906 as well as making many men redundant. In 1914 the Blaenau men were

exhorted to join up, and their colleagues were put on a three-day
week. Men moved from the area to the mines of South Wales and
the slate towns became empty. In Bethesda 'shops have now few
customers, 1,400 men are away. Misery and privation are present in
hundreds of the quarrymen's houses.' In 1971 the Oakeley quarry
closed. At the time of closure it was the biggest slate mine in the
world with nearly 50 miles of underground caverns and pathways.
In 1972, however, it was re-opened on a reduced scale, together
with a museum and visitor centre. The open section, Gloddfa
Gonal, the middle mine, is now a major tourist attraction with visits
underground where tableaux indicate the old mining methods. On
the opposite side of the A470, at this stage rising over the Crimea
pass, is the Llechwedd mine, one of the pioneers of the
mechanisation of the slate industry. Here electricity was introduced
for the first time in 1890, one of its first advantages being to cut the
drilling time of powder holes from 10 hours to $1\frac{1}{2}$ minutes.
Llechwedd never actually closed, though now it too is chiefly a
tourist attraction, including an electric tranway tour through the
caverns.

Whether or not the wayfarer visits the slate quarries or, indeed,
Blaenau Ffestiniog itself he must eventually reach the centre of
Tan-y-Grisiau village (687451). From there take the road going
west and follow it up towards the hills. At the waterfalls on the
stream draining down from Llyn Cwmorthin go west and up into the
Moelwyns. When south of Moel-yr-hydd (672455) the wayfarer has
a choice. He can go north of west on a route for Cwm Croesor, or he
can go south of west for Moelwyn Mawr. He should do the latter.
Moelwyn Mawr is a fine peak offering excellent views in all
directions and can be descended by the ridge running almost due
west that is one of the most classical in form in the whole of Wales
when viewed from its base at, say, (640446). Continue down to the
road and go right into Croesor.

Croesor
It is perhaps naïve to write or say that one place typifies an area or
a country, particularly in a country such as Wales whose essence

Cnicht and Moelwyn Mawr from the south-west

seems to be diversity. That said, the first view of Croesor village
does capture, in a single view, something that is North Wales.
There, in a valley that is not gentle, particularly in winter, hemmed
in by hills which dwarf it in a way that emphasises the smallness of
man in the mountains, is a village of a few houses and a chapel. The
scar of a quarry can be seen on the hillside but it has long since
closed so that the secluded, private community has ebbed away.
This is the land of the holiday home that has brought an untimely
end to the Welshness of the villages. There was talk of damming the
valley not many years ago and flooding it for a pump-storage power
plant. But despite the attempts to remove it from the map Croesor
lives on. The village received some transient fame in the years
around the Second World War because of a remarkable inhabitant,
Bob Owen, who was so much a part of the village that he was known
as Bob Owen Croesor. Bob was born in 1885 and raised in the

village of Llanfrothen, a slightly bigger village than Croesor and about 2 miles away. His memory of his upbringing, by his grandmother, would make a chapter in a history of social anthropology. The cottage was one-storey, but the beds were four-posters. Grandmother salted down two pigs annually for food and was an expert with herbs. Bob's schooling was, to his eternal regret, in English and of the English Empire. It had few advantages in a Welsh-speaking community when you wished to know the names of Welsh heroes and mountains. His first job was as a farm labourer but his quick brain was noted and he became clerk to the quarry at Croesor. As a farmhand he slept with the other hands in the stable loft and recalled that snow and rain came through the unfelted slate roof to soak them at night, and that the only drying facility they had was the warmth rising from the horses. He, and many others, suffered rheumatism and arthritis in later years because of this. As clerk to the quarry for 30 years his only memory was of being deputed by the 'absent' manager to tell the men on Saturday that the quarry had closed for good that day and that everyone, himself included, was unemployed. But for all this Bob Owen never gave up his ambition to be a book collector and reader. He collected and read widely, and by the 1930's was a recognised expert on many aspects of Welsh history. In recognition of this expertise he was awarded an honorary MA from the University of Wales in 1931. At that time his library was around 20,000 books and was of great interest and some value. By the time of his death in 1962, at the age of 77, it had risen to around 50,000 volumes. In the years following the war he became a minor celebrity and had many radio and TV appearances to his credit.

Bob's writings are sparse but are touched with the poetry of the Welsh hills. The author never met him, indeed was hardly a contemporary. But to read him and of him is to admire him, not in the patronising way that the press of the day referred to him as a self-educated quarryman, but as a man unbound by the apparent brutishness of his early years, completely at one with his life. That last quality is, perhaps, the gift of villages such as Croesor – the way they can offer a glimpse of a truer sense of values.

Also in Croesor is Ffynnon Helen, Helen's spring. This is named

from Princess Helen, who may also have given her name to Sarn Helen, Helen's Causeway, the Roman road that traverses Wales. Helen is reputed to have married the Emperor Maximus and persuaded him to build the causeway so that her people could travel more easily. Helen travelled often with her husband's legion, and one day she was on her way from Segontium (Caernarfon) south towards Ffestiniog when she stopped here, where there then was no village but a cool spring. Her party was in two halves, a second group being commanded by her youngest and favourite son. The story is that as her son passed Castell Cidwm to the west of Snowdon the giant Cidwm emerged from this castle and killed him. The truth, if there is any grain of truth in the story at all, is more likely that the boy was killed by his jealous older brother. A courier rushed on to tell the princess the sad news and when told she cried out in despair, 'Oh, Croesawr, oh, cursed hour'. From then on the spring was known as Ffynnon Helen, but the site was called Croesor.

The spring is to the right of our route up past the chapel, and that way also is Cnicht, the Matterhorn of Wales, a low mountain at only 2,265 feet, but of exquisite appearance from this view. Sadly the summit is, in fact, a ridge running away from Croesor so that from all other sides, and the summit, the illusion is destroyed. Interestingly the elegant name is not Welsh, but English, the name for a knight's helmet or cnight, probably given by sailors viewing the peak from Cardigan Bay.

Leave Croesor along the lane going north-west, and follow this to Bwlchgwernog (612452), reversing the route of the woeful queen. From here a quiet lane leads to Nantmor, a village whose name, from Nant-y-mor – the stream by the sea – gives a clue to the ancient position of the sea near these land-locked acres. A further clue, to those of course who do not know the history of the area mentioned before in reference to Porthmadog, is in the name of our next, and one of the major, highspots on the route – Aberglaslyn.

An eighteenth-century visitor after visiting the pass stated, 'How shall I express my feelings! The dark tremendous precipices, the rapid river roaring over disjointed rocks, black caverns, and issuing

Aberglaslyn pass

cataracts; all serve to make this the noblest specimen of the Finely Horrid the eye can possibly behold; the Poet has not described, nor the Painter pictured so gloomy a retreat, 'tis the last approach to the mansion of Pluto through the regions of Despair.' It is difficult to understand such folly now, when we see incomparable beauty where he saw the finely horrid. The separation between ourselves and that writer is 200 years, and two states of mind. Aberglaslyn may not be the masterpiece that it has on occasions been made out to be, but it is undoubtedly a very beautiful place, particularly in spring and autumn when summer's crowds and winter's bareness are gone. The name recalls that this point was at the river mouth before Madocks built his Cob and reclaimed the estuary.

To savour the delights of the pass, take the path on the east side of the river. This assumes that the wayfarer has reached the bridge on the A4085 (595462) from Nantmor. The intrepid can actually follow the old railway line from Nantmor through the tunnels, which are dark and wet, but not full of pits. The path along the Glaslyn leads to Beddgelert.

Beddgelert

Beddgelert is one of the most famous of the Snowdonia villages and is a honey-pot for tourists. The legend behind Gelert's grave beside the pathway a little to the south of the village is well known. Llywelyn the Great had a faithful dog, Gelert, who accompanied him on all his hunting trips, but one day stayed at home while his master hunted. A wolf came into the prince's home and seeing the prince's son in his cradle he made for him only to be intercepted by Gelert. In the furious fight that followed the wolf was killed, Gelert was wounded and covered with blood and the cradle was overturned, the blankets falling on the blood-stained floor. Llywelyn returned and was horrified to be greeted by the bloodied dog. He hurried indoors and seeing the blood-stained blankets and overturned cradle became convinced that the dog had killed his son. He instantly drew his sword and stabbed the dog whose dying yell woke the baby asleep under the blankets. Only then was the wolf's body found and Llywelyn realised how faithful the dog had been.

His remorse was keen, and he buried the dog with full honours beneath a fine cairn. It is a good story, but it is not now Beddgelert got its name.

The story itself is an ancient one, the first version being in Sanskrit, and the Welsh version probably pre-dates Llywelyn. It may have been transferred to him because of his own dog, for there is reason to believe that King John gave Llywelyn a deer-hunting dog called Killhart. Beddgelert is possibly named from a holy man, Celert, who lived in a hermit's cell in the area in Norman times. There is also evidence that an Irish chieftan called Celert lived in the area, or at least visited his children who lived here. There again there was a group of Celtic monks called Celei who may have had a house in the area. The only certainty is that 'Bedd' means grave. The idea of transferring the legend of Llywelyn's dog Gelert to the area appears to have been the brainchild of one David Prichard, the owner of the *Royal Goat* hotel who certainly had a motive for the deed. That piece of information alone may make all other speculation redundant, for there is evidence that the old village was called Llanyborth, the church of the port, when boats reached Aberglaslyn. It makes little difference now. The legend is a good tale, its only sad side-effect being the number of people who only visit the 'grave' and do not recognise the great beauty that is everywhere in the village. As one visitor put it –

Pass on O tender hearted. Dry your eyes.
Not here a greyhound but a landlord lies.

The village is placed strategically at the meeting-point of the rivers Glaslyn and Colwyn, and was the site of one of the earliest monasteries in Wales. Indeed it is likely that only the house on the holy island of Bardsey pre-dates Beddgelert's Augustinian Priory. In one form or another the house existed from the sixth century but was endowed by Llywelyn the Great's grandson, Llywelyn the Last, in true medieval fashion in the early thirteenth century. In the years that followed it was burnt down, as were so many others, on the odd occasion, but survived until the Dissolution. Nothing now remains, although the church retains some of the original priory church.

Elsewhere the village is idyllic though it can be overpopulated and sadly the old bridge, itself so picturesque, is a nightmare when filled with holiday coaches. The visitor who wants to see the village properly must be very patient, or must come in winter.

To continue, the east, later south, bank of the Glaslyn is followed back to Llyn Dinas. At (606492) on the northern side of the river is Dinas Emrys, fortress of Vortigern, the King of the Britons who failed to halt the Saxon invasion of Britain. The site has Iron Age and early medieval aspects to its true history, but it is to legend that we look for the most interesting and significant details. When the Saxons invaded, carrying all before them, Vortigern asked his magicians what he should do to save himself and they told him to build a tower, which he decided to do, here at Dinas Emrys. His masons set to work, but every morning they found that the previous day's work had disappeared into the earth. Desperately Vortigern consulted the magicians again, and they told him he must find a boy with no father who should be killed at the spot. When the earth was soaked with his blood the tower could stand. Messengers went far and wide and eventually found a boy whose mother was a royal princess who had been made pregnant by an invisible and, therefore, unknown being – an incubus demon, half man, half angel. They took the boy to Vortigern but before he could be sacrificed he accused the magicians of false prophecy claiming that the tower disappeared because of what was under it. Impressed by his manner Vortigern followed the boy's suggestion, digging into the ground to reveal an underwater pool. The pool was drained and there, as the boy predicted, were two sleeping dragons, one red and one white. The dragons woke and began to fight, the fighting following the prophecies of the boy. First the white dragon was winning, but then the red dragon recovered and beat him away, but just as it was about to kill the white it started instead to tear itself apart. There were more and detailed prophecies, for the boy was Merlin, later magician to King Arthur. This version of the fight of the dragons is believed to be correct, and is thought to parallel the fight between the British (Welsh), the red dragon, and the Saxons, the white dragon. In that case it is largely accurate, for the Saxons won until the time of Arthur, then lost badly only to see internal factions in

Nantgwynant

the British camp give it the upper hand again following Arthur's death. Later writers saw the battle as Welsh against Norman or Englishman and re-wrote the battle scene with the red dragon winning, but Merlin's prophecy was never actually proved false. The tale itself is fascinating because it ties in with an even earlier one, given in the Mabinogion, of Lludd, King of Britain, who buried dragons at a spot in Eryri to rid Britain of a plague of screaming. Again the dragons were red and white, but in the earlier tale they were found at Oxford, on the invasion route of the Saxon armies.

Those who would like a closer look at Dinas Emrys can cross the footbridge at (604489), but the fort is on private land. The alternative route is to follow the southern shore of Llyn Dinas on a track heading for the minor road at (627502). The view northward on the path is excellent, the dark lake and the mountains beyond.

That southward is interesting for those seeing it for the first time, the long ridge to the south-east being Cnicht, which is only Matterhorn-shaped from the Porthmadog side.

The route crosses the Glaslyn to emerge on the A498 at (626503). Go right to the start of the Watkin path at (627506), and follow this northward.

Eryri

Eryri is the Welsh name for this northern part of the Snowdonia National Park, the part that contains the highest Welsh peak, Yr Wyddfa or Snowdon. So often has the name been translated as land of eagles that it is heretical to challenge it, but it should be noted that there have been different explanations of the name. George Borrow, for instance, maintained that the name could have signified an 'excrescence or scrofulous eruption' (!) or jagged, rocky hills as we might say. As regards eagles, certainly they existed in the mountains up until a few centuries ago. In the days of Giraldus they were relatively common, although he does not specifically maintain that 'Eryri' derived from them. Giraldus also states that one remarkable eagle lived in Snowdonia (one bird or one type?), which perched on a particular stone every fifth feast day to be ready to eat the bodies of dead men as it knew that on that day war would break out. He declares that the stone had a hole in it worn by the sharpening of the bird's beak, and to make the story more credible points out that the eagle knows the place it can find its prey, but not the time, while the raven knows the time, but not the place.

Until the latter half of the eighteenth century, i.e. before the slate industry, this area was truly wild with no roads and few tracks. As late as the early nineteenth century the original transport system, the horse-drawn sled, could still be seen, towing 3-hundredweight loads along the pony tracks. The houses were poor and conditions primitive. The livestock shared the house, cows being at one end and people at the other, with the heating a central fire below a hole in the roof. In front of the fire there would frequently be a pig happily curled up, oblivious to the sinister significance of sage and onion. Today there is access in plenty and Eryri is feeling the presence of people. It has things that are irreplaceable, the

Snowdon lily, an arctic spider that lives nowhere else, even wild (feral) goats. But mainly it has peace, a rare quality. Frequently the peace is shattered by the tourist hordes. The keen or expert walker can always find his peace by moving to a different area or just moving farther into the hills. But we should all beware. Erosion and pollution are not just a product of the car-borne day tripper, as rubbish in the remoter areas shows. Dr. Johnson, a good few years ago, defined the mountaineer as a 'freebooter or savage'. Today his definition holds good for too many of the breed.

The Watkin path was presented to the nation for public use by Sir Edward Watkin, the railway magnate, in 1892. To open the path Watkin persuaded prime minister Gladstone down from Caernarfon on 13 September. Gladstone, the Grand Old Man as he was known even then, was 84 and in his fourth term as prime minister. It was a vile day with pouring rain, but he and his wife travelled in an open car to acknowledge the cheers of the crowd. A great many people then walked, still in rain, to a rostrum where there was hymn singing and speech making. Gladstone spoke on the 'Land Question in Wales' and enjoyed the singing very much, asking for several encores. There were cheers and the throng departed. Not one word was mentioned about the path, which since the whole thing was staged for its opening is a little sad. To make amends Sir Edward and Lady Watkin, the Gladstones and a few others followed the path the next day. Only Lady Watkin and a friend reached the summit, though many made Bwlch y Saethau. Mrs. Gladstone used a donkey and there were many who wished that the Grand Old Man had used it. This was due to an assault on Gladstone by a cow at Chester a little earlier. After the assault the cow was butchered and sold at a high price, the hide was stuffed and exhibited and her calf fetched good money. Many felt that if a cow which tried to kill him was worth so much then a donkey which had helped him might be worth even more!

We follow in the footsteps of those who made it to Bwlch y Saethau and we also see the tremendous view of Glaslyn that opens up. Bwlch y Saethau is the pass of the arrows. This is the legendary site of King Arthur's last battle when he fought together with the few knights of the Round Table still loyal to him against Mordred,

who had plotted to overthrow him, renegade knights and a Saxon
army which Mordred had persuaded to help him by offering to
divide up Arthur's Britain. In that last great battle the most
enduring legend is of Arthur hacking a path through the enemy
lines until he came face to face with Mordred. Mordred, the
younger man, struck first and Arthur received a death wound, but
Excalibur flashed once more in his hand and Mordred was hit so
hard that his helmet was cleaved open and his head split deep. As
hero and villain should, Arthur fell quietly while Mordred fell
screaming. The name here derives from another version of the
story, in which Arthur is struck down by a lucky arrow as the Saxon
hordes retreated. Either way Arthur lay dying on the pass and was
carried by Sir Bedivere down to the shores of Llyn Llydaw below Y
Lliwedd. There Bedivere and other knights sat weeping beside the
silent body of their King, when Arthur opened his eyes and told
Bedivere to stop crying and to take Excalibur and cast it into the
lake beyond the ridge. Legend has it that this lake was Llyn Idwal
beyond the Glyder ridge, which is surely too far even for a
superhero. Bedivere took the sword, but could not throw it away
because of its beauty, and so he hid it away and returned to Arthur.
The King asked him what he had seen and when Bedivere replied
nothing he swore at him as a liar and sent him away again. Again
Bedivere hid the sword and returned and again he was reviled, now
as a traitor and a liar. A third time Bedivere went and this time he
threw the sword into the middle of the lake where a hand rose and
caught it, waved it three times and disappeared. When told Arthur
was content and lay quietly. Then a black boat came from out of the
mist over Llyn Llydaw and three ladies in it took the King and
ferried him into the mist again. Sir Bedivere stood up and cried out
in despair, 'What will become of me now?' Arthur replied that he
was going to Avalon to have his wound healed and that when
Britain needed him he would come again. Then as the boat
disappeared from view a low, sad cry came floating across the lake.

   Sir Bedivere took the last of the knights that remained and went
into a cave in the cliffs below Y Lliwedd to await the call. Years
later a shepherd wandering on the cliff in search of lost sheep found
the cave entrance and went in. When he lit a match to see where he

was he was amazed to see a circle of knights asleep on the cave floor, each in armour with a sword ready at his side, and in the middle an old man in a gold crown lying on a couch with a great sword with a jewelled handle by his side. The shepherd stepped back in amazement and his head hit a bell in the doorway. It rang once, echoing in the cave, and the old King awoke. 'Is it time?' he asked and the shepherd shouted, 'No, sleep on'. The King looked at him, nodded and said, 'Then I will sleep on until I shall rise to bring victory to my people in Britain.' And he slept again. The shepherd hurried away and though he often tried he could never again find the cave in the cliff face.

Since we are talking of Y Lliwedd it is worth noting that one way of reaching Pen-y-Pass is to go over Y Lliwedd from here and continue along the Miner's track. That offers the excellent view of Yr Wyddfa from over Llyn Llydaw. One Victorian mountaineer from Wales was once heard to comment during a climb on the Jungfrau that the view to the Bernese Oberland was fine. Indeed, he said, it was almost as good as that of Yr Wyddfa over Llydaw, though spoiled by the quantity of snow. To take in that view, however, the wayfarer would have to forgo Yr Wyddfa's summit, so resolve to do the Snowdon horseshoe one day (see below) and go to Yr Wyddfa.

Yr Wyddfa

The highest point of the range, and the highest peak in England and Wales, is commonly known as Snowdon. In Welsh it is Yr Wyddfa, the grave, though this name should be correctly applied only to the summit mound which is reputedly the grave of the giant Rhita, Rhita Gawr, Anglicised occasionally to Rhito Gigas. Rhita was renowned as the collector of the beards of famous people, but one day he overreached himself and tried to cut off Arthur's beard. Incensed, Arthur sliced off the giant's head and the body fell here where in time it became covered to form the 'grave' we see today. Yr Wyddfa can justifiably claim to be the finest mountain in England and Wales, with its cliffs, ridges and lakes. From almost any angle it is near perfect, but the finest prospect is from the east with the steep cliff of Clogwyn y Garnedd rising above Glaslyn.

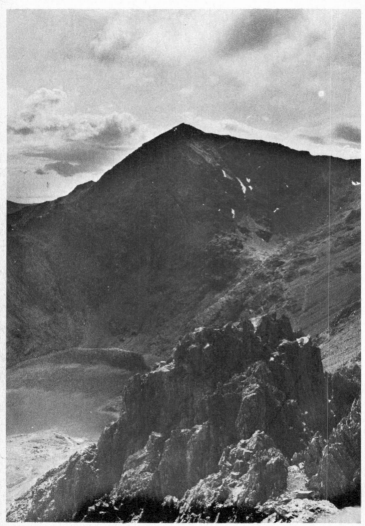

Yr Wyddfa from the pinnacles on Crib Goch

From the summit on a clear day the visitor may see the Lake
District, Scottish hills and the Wicklow mountains in Ireland. The
ridge walk that links the three 3,000-foot peaks, Crib Goch,
Crib-y-ddisgl and Yr Wyddfa, and continues over Y Lliwedd to
make the Snowdon horseshoe, is arguably the finest in Wales and
must be included in the itinerary of anyone wanting to be
considered a mountain walker. From the summit of Yr Wyddfa the
wayfarer could take the train, built in only 13 months in the late
1890's on a gauge of 2 ft $7\frac{1}{2}$ in. It is almost 5 miles long and has, in
fact, a relatively shallow gradient despite a rack-and-pinion drive.
Alternatively the wayfarer must choose one of two routes, either
the low-level route following the zig-zag paths down the pyg track
(p. 229) or down again to the Miner's track along the lakesides, or
the high-level route over the remaining two 3,000-foot peaks,
descending directly to Pen-y-pass from Crib Goch. The former is a
fine low-level route with excellent views of the Lliwedd cliffs. If the
Miner's track is followed then both the Snowdon lakes are passed.
The first lake below Snowdon is Glaslyn, the blue lake, whose more
correct, and older, name is Llyn Ffynnon Las, the lake of the blue
spring. Here there lives the Welsh equivalent of the Loch Ness
Monster, the Afanc, which occasionally – but only very, very
occasionally! – surfaces to frighten the daylights out of a passing
wayfarer. The Afanc lived initially in a pool in the Conwy river
where he made a perpetual nuisance of himself by using his
supernatural powers to flood the area when the mood took him,
ruining crops and drowning animals. Many had tried to kill him but
his scales could not be pierced by arrows and few had lived to tell
the story of their failure. Finally it was decided to use the Afanc's
liking for beautiful young girls to lure him to a trap. A brave girl sat
on the pool edge and the Afanc, suitably interested, dragged himself
out on to the bank and laid his huge and horrible head on her lap.
Men appeared from everywhere and the Afanc was chained up
thrashing all the time at the men with his huge clawed feet and
biting at the chains. Two huge oxen were brought from
Betws-y-Coed and they began to haul the Afanc towards Snowdon.
The effort was great, so great that at one spot, above Llyn Gwynant,
an eye from one of the oxen fell out. The tears shed to cleanse the

Crib Goch above the causeway on the Miner's track

socket formed the Ox's Eye Pool – Llygad yr Ych. Eventually,
however, Glaslyn was reached and the Afanc was dumped in, the
chains having been relaxed. The creature seems to have realised it
was beaten because it never used its supernatural powers for
revenge, or to move back to the Conwy, and in Glaslyn it lives still.

The legend is a very satisfying one, because it shows the link
between truth, suitably exaggerated, and myth. At one time there
really was an Afanc, but not the crocodile-like creature of the
legend, the real one was a beaver. Usually in Welsh the beaver was
'llostlydan', the broad-tailed one, but was also known as 'efync' or
water-monster. The monster idea seems to have been derived from
a great flood in the Conwy valley caused by the breaking of a beaver
lodge dam under the weight of winter water. This would also
explain the malicious flooding of the area by the Afanc, that
appears in the story. At one time the beaver could be found in any
of the wooded valleys of Wales, but its fur and meat, and the ease
with which it could be killed during its hibernation sleep, meant that
it became extinct in a relatively short time after the mountain areas
of Wales became inhabited. By the time of Hywel Dda, the early
tenth century, a beaver pelt was worth 15 ox hides, suggesting that
by then the beaver was scarce. Giraldus tells us, in 1198, that there
were no beavers in North Wales, though he maintains that there still
were some in the Teifi. Clearly the story of the flood in the Conwy
valley caused by a water monster became exaggerated in the years
following the animal's extinction. It is interesting and at the same
time sad that such stories should be so readily explained. Of course
as late as the nineteenth century a man fishing in the lake attached
himself to something that surfaced giving him a glimpse of head and
jaws, and he didn't stop running until he reached Beddgelert . . .

The ridge from Yr Wyddfa takes in the famous pinnacles beyond
Bwlch Moch on its way to Crib Goch. The name Bwlch Moch is
strange, as moch means pig. This seems to tie in with the track
below, the pig track, but the form of that track is usually pyg not pig,
and moch could also mean soon or quick, making the pass the quick
way which makes better sense than any reference to pigs. Pyg could
then be P-y-G from *Pen y Gwyrd*, the inn beyond Pen-y-Pass.

All routes reach Pen-y-Pass at the head of the Llanberis pass

The Llanberis pass from the pinnacles on Crib Goch

where 'A perpetual unbroken sabbath stillness reigns through the vast profound, except that at intervals, the piercing cry of the kite or the hawk, the hoarse and discordant note of the raven, or the wild minstrelsy of the stream is heard.'

Go down the path a few yards for access to the Glyders range. The name derives, almost certainly, from cludr, a heap or pile, a root that gives us also clitter on Dartmoor and glidder in Southern Scotland, each meaning a rock pile. The name is appropriate for the summit area of Glyder Fach.

The Glyders offer some of the most interesting and diverse scenery of any small area in Wales. Between the summits of Glyder Fawr and Glyder Fach is Castell y Gwynt, the castle of the winds, a jumble of huge rock slabs which is at the same time both bizarre and yet in no way incongruous. On Glyder Fach the rock slab piles are repeated, here with the added touch of a cantilevered slab which has, to date, lasted the test of time. Charles Kingsley wrote of the

Y Garn from Tryfan

summit region – 'that enormous desolation, the dead bones of the
eldest born of time', and of the cantilever – 'a line of obelisks like
giants crouching side by side'.

From Glyder Fach the Bristly Ridge leads down to Bwlch Tryfan
which separates the main Glyder mass from Tryfan. The Glyder
range stretches northward to Elidar Fawr and Carnedd y Filiast, the
former offering views of the lower Llanberis pass, the latter of the
beautiful Nant Francon, as the lower valley between the Glyders
and the Carneddau is known. But the interest is drawn towards
Tryfan which is a peak for the connoisseur. On its summit there are
two standing stones named, for no good reason, Adam and Eve.
The stones are, in fact, the top sections of parallel igneous ribs, from
which the softer rock has weathered. The truth is mundane, the
possibility of a supernatural erection is better, and the freedom of
Tryfan offered to those who take the risky step between the two
worth striving for.

Snowdon, Glyder Fawr and the Castle of the Winds, from Glyder Fach

As on Snowdon the wayfarer is spoilt for choice, Glyder Fawr, Glyder Fach and Tryfan, the Cribin ridge. As good as any is to climb Glyder Fawr and then descend to the head of Twll Du, the Devil's Kitchen, a cleft in the hillside. To descend now the path *must* be followed as it goes down the south side (right side from above) of the cleft. The walker is now in Cwm Idwal, the lake of which is the centre of a natural nature reserve. The plant life of the boggy margin of the lake includes the insectivorous sundew. The lake is also Idwal, named after the son of Owain Gwynedd, reputedly drowned here by his foster parents.

Continue past the Idwal slabs to the head of Nant Francon. To traverse the Carneddau ahead the wayfarer must now climb Pen-yr-ole-wen, perhaps the steepest walking route in Wales. Cross the Alf Embleton stile (649605), a fine memorial to this treasurer of the Ramblers' Association, discreetly engraved, and start. The climb is about 650 metres at about 1 in 2, its only real advantage

Tryfan and the Afon Ogwen

being that once over you stay up for good, the Carneddau being a
series of whaleback ridges all around the same height. The two
highest peaks, that give the range its name, are Carnedd Dafydd
and Carnedd Llywelyn named for Llywelyn ap Gruffydd and his
brother Dafydd. Both of these, and Foel Grach and Foel Fras, are
crossed naturally in a traverse of the range. Only Yr Elen of the
Carneddau 3,000-foot peaks is missed and that can be included if
the wayfarer has a will. There are 14 peaks in Snowdonia over
3,000 feet high, three on Snowdon, five on the Glyders, and six
here. The climb over all of these in 24 hours is a well-known
test-piece. The suggested route here covers half of them, and
represents a very reasonable attempt for a back-packer.

From Foel Fras, a disappointing peak with a trig. point set in a
stony plateau much of which seems higher and bounded by a wall
that almost certainly is, the route goes over Drum (709696) and on
to Bwlch y Ddeufaen (717717). Even though the Carneddau is

Yr Elen from the east

losing height now as it falls off towards the sea and the Conwy valley, the interest is maintained with fine views here, and excellent walking north-east to the Sychnant Pass (748770).

Sychnant means dry stream, an accurate description of the valley but hardly one that conveys the elegance of the pass. It is a miniature of the bigger passes, but that helps, the mind being allowed to cope with it at one go. Cross the pass at its head for the signed path to Conwy mountain. The elegance of form can be seen to perfection here. It is hardly surprising that Sychnant is depicted on many postcards offering the finest passes in North Wales.

On Conwy mountain is Castell Caer Leion (759779), a Roman fort with a name linking this spot, symbolically almost in view of our journey, with that of the same name in South Wales. The reason for the fort's existence can clearly be seen, the mountain dominating the Conwy estuary and being naturally defended on all sides.

Go east along the ridge towards the town, reaching it at (775778) where a lane leads the wayfarer to his terminal town.

The Sychnant pass

Conwy

As a finishing point to a major walk through, and an investigation of, Wales there could be few better choices, at sea level, than the town of Conwy. It could be argued that Caernarfon, with its more imposing and symmetrical castle and its royal connections, is a fine end-point, but Caernarfon does not have the charm of Conwy, the little walled town with its castle, river and railway bridges. In Welsh the town is Conwy, dropping the offending 'a' of the English Conway, or Aberconwy which accurately positions it, where the river meets the sea. There was, as we have seen, an Iron Age hill-fort on the mountain above the town, and at a later date a fortification on Deganwy mountain on the eastern side of the estuary. Between the two the Romans had an interest here, as the oyster beds at Penarth, on the river a little to the south of the castle, yielded good pearls. Suetonius claims that the chief motive for the

Roman invasion of Britain was the pearl fisheries, and while this is undoubtedly of dubious veracity it is certainly true that Julius Caesar had a breast-plate made set with pearls from Britain for a temple gift. Today the oyster beds still yield the occasional small pearl.

The first recorded inhabitants on this western river bank were Cistercian monks who set up the abbey of Aberconwy in the last quarter of the twelfth century. The abbey was obviously important as it received official recognition of its founding, and a setting out of its boundaries, from Llywelyn the Great himself. That Llywelyn was capable of such a gesture to the monks is proof of the independent existence of the state of Wales at the time. Problems were to follow shortly after, however, as the marcher lords looked covetously at the Welsh lands. Inevitably the Conwy river became a natural boundary between the westward-pushing Normans and the Welsh, and in 1211 an English army camped on Deganwy mountain. Here they found the remains of the original fort, constructed by Maelgwyn, King of Gwynedd, on the conspicuous twin mounds of the mountain top. The river itself proved a formidable obstacle however and the army retreated. In 1245 another attempt was made. This time an English soldier noted – 'there is a small arm of the sea (that) lies between us and Snowdon, where the Welsh quarter themselves, and is, at high tide, about a crossbow-shot wide.' That small distance was sufficient to prevent any massive incursion by the English though one raiding party, at least, crossed the river and attacked the abbey itself, stealing the plate and books and firing the house. A final period of relative peace descended on the area until the coming of Edward Plantagenet, the castle builder. Shortly before his accession to the throne Llewelyn ap Grufydd sacked Deganwy castle making it imperative that any invading army should construct another. Edward saw immediately that the continued existence of the Conwy as a defensive barrier was to the advantage of the Welsh and so he crossed it and constructed the present castle at Conwy itself. The building started in 1283, the same year as construction started at Harlech and Caernarfon. Since the town was now to be garrisoned, the existence of the monks on the site was an embarrassment. It is also possible that the monks

Conwy

may have been seen as a threat to the site's security, owing, as they did, so much to the princes of Gwynedd and being no great lovers of the invaders following the earlier sacrilege. Edward was duly reverent of the brethren, however, seeking the consent of the Pope to re-site the monastery. The consent was granted, the abbey being informed that 'your Monastery for many reasonable causes could not remain conveniently in the place where it then was'. The monks were therefore resettled on a site about 7 miles up-river near Llanrwst. Nothing of Aberconwy abbey now survives, except in the oldest parts of the parish church, which was the abbey church.

Following removal of the monks from the site, the castle and the town walls were built, in the remarkably short time of four years, under the direction of James of St. George, Master of the King's Works in Wales. He was the greatest military architect of the time and was brought over from France to help defend Edward's newly conquered lands. To accomplish the work in so short a time a workforce of 1,500 was employed, the cost of the project being about £15,000. This latter figure is, in present-day terms, about £5 million, and though such comparisons can be misleading it does give a feel for the size of the undertaking, and the relative cheapness of the labour force who were, in modern terms, being paid about £1,000 per year and finding their own stone out of that. The castle and the town walls were constructed as a single entity with the castle itself forming the strongest point, positioned in the south-east corner on an outcrop of rock. Before the construction of the two rail bridges which cross the river from the very walls themselves, almost as drawbridges, the castle must have been a formidable sight from across the river. It is of a relatively straightforward design with an inner ward separated from an outer ward by a wall and drawbridge. The concentric design proven at Caerphilly 20 years before was not used because of the restricted site. The wards were protected by eight more or less symmetrically placed towers, and the whole was further strengthened by the presence of east and west barbicans, the east allowing provisioning from a watergate on the river, the west connecting with the town by a drawbridge over a moat.

The town walls are a little under a mile in length, with three main gates and 21 defensive towers, all of which are, to a lesser or greater extent, intact, and the walk around the walls is a delightful lap of honour for the successful wayfarer. The three main gates still exist, Porth Uchaf – the upper gate leading out into Gwynedd, towards the castle at Caernarfon; Porth y Felin – the mill gate opening out towards the town's mill on the Gyffin stream; and Porth Isaf – the lower gate leading to the beach. As the beach was itself fortified, with the castle at one end and a spur wall and tower at the northern end, this was the way that the majority of provisions arrived. The castle was virtually siege-proof as was proved very early. On his second visit to the castle – his first having been on the way to Caernarfon castle where, in 1284, his son, the first English Prince of Wales, was born – in late 1294, Edward I was marooned by the rebellion of Madoc ap Llewelyn. As the castle's provisions decreased the King and his men watched the floodwaters of the River Conwy which prevented all attempts to resupply the castle from the sea. Thankfully for the beleaguered troops spring brought good weather and the ships arrived. The record states that the King celebrated a belated Christmas in the castle Great Hall. As part of the festivities a collection of Welsh bards, believed by Edward to be behind the rebellion, were executed in the town. Only one escaped this summary fate, by leaping from the castle into the river where he was killed instantly.

The wall towers are placed at roughly 50-yard intervals and are not integral with the wall, there being no continuous walkway from each wall section past a tower to the next section. The gap across the tower throat was normally bridged by planking that did allow continuous walking. The idea was that the wall itself represented a formidable barrier, but should it be topped the captured section could be isolated from other sections by removing the tower planking. The attacker then could continue only by taking the hazardous leap into the town and its waiting defenders. Meanwhile the still-controlled wall sections on each side of the captured section could be used by archers firing at invaders scaling the captured wall. It was a very simple, but highly effective, defence method. At night, and in times of unrest, the planking was left in place, the battlements being continuously patrolled.

Following the siege of Edward I in 1294 the castle had a quiet century, but saw brief action in 1399 when Richard II stayed here on his way from Ireland towards England and the rebellion of Henry, Duke of Lancaster, later Henry IV. An emissary arrived from Henry to persuade the King to go peaceably to Flint for a meeting, and was believed when he swore on the Bible in the castle chapel that there was no trickery. Convinced, Richard made off with only a small group of men but when he reached Colwyn Bay he was ambushed. We learn that 'when he saw the ambushes he was sore abashed, knowing well he was betrayed . . . for he was in such a place as he could not escape'. Richard was indeed captured and, later, died at the hands of his enemy.

The castle was again in action in 1401, this time very strangely as it was captured in an entirely bloodless campaign. The reason for this lay in the medieval rules of chivalry which the English still obeyed. To them war was the highest form of gaming, governed by a strict moral code that was imposed, in part, by the church. The fundamental rule was, therefore, that there should be no war on Sundays or holy days. The commander of the garrison at Conwy, John Massey, recognised this and on Easter Sunday, 1401 – that was also, ironically, 1 April – he left the castle with a nominal guard of two men and marched the rest of the garrison, a total of 73 soldiers and archers, to church in the town. Unfortunately Massey was not confronted this time by a chivalrous European army who also knew the rules of war, but by a group of followers of Owain Glyndwr led by two brothers from Anglesey. They were Gwilym and Rhys Tewdwr, members of an important family whose descendants would later be kings of England, but who were now rebels against the throne. As soon as the garrison had departed a man dressed as, and claiming to be, a carpenter approached the castle gates. The two remaining guards let him in and seconds later they were dead, the castle being occupied by Gwilym Tewdwr and about 40 rebels, his brother Rhys occupying high ground above the town. The rebels then fired the town and destroyed all the castle's, and therefore most of North Wales', records. By the time Massey reached the castle, bewildered by the holy day campaign, it was all over – the town was gutted, the castle taken. When news reached Henry Percy, the famed Hotspur, Chief Justice of North Wales and Massey's superior, he was understandably shocked. He gathered a small army and marched on Conwy. Massey was arrested and the castle besieged. There had to be a quick end to the siege. Clearly the rebels could not hold out for ever; but equally the English could not afford the Welsh, and the English in Wales, to get the impression that uprisings of this kind could succeed – they needed a quick recapture of the castle and punishment of the rebels. Negotiations between Percy and the Tewdwrs dragged on for over a month. The Tewdwrs wanted free pardons for all inside the castle, Percy and his King wanted them all dead. At last a compromise was reached, one so unpleasant that everyone was appalled by it, and that in an age when life was cheap. The Welsh bound nine of their number 'by stealth as they slept after the night watches', and gave them up on condition of saving their own and others' lives. And so, on 28 May 1401, the rest of the castle rebels walked free as nine of their

number were 'drawn, disembowelled, hanged, beheaded and quartered'. It certainly seems that Percy was executing all Welshmen in the guise of these nine. The disgrace of his hollow victory stayed with him, and the treachery of the Welsh to their own fellows also seems to have stayed with the campaigners throughout the Glyndwr rebellion.

Conwy's involvement with the Civil War was strange. A famous son – John Williams, Archbishop of York, a convinced Royalist – returned home from York when the Parliamentarian army moved north. Finding the castle in a sorry state of disrepair, he had it restored using money from his own pocket. The restoration was obviously successful, a Parliamentarian army under General Mytton being stopped in the summer of 1646. By that time, however, the Royalist cause was collapsing and there was a lot of bad feeling between the King's supporters. Conwy's governor insulted Williams, who promptly changed sides and joined the siege of his own handiwork. The town fell in August, but the castle held out till November despite a considerable battering that left it ruined. The Parliamentarians treated the Welsh defenders of the castle very honourably, as befitted their bravery, but were less well inclined to a group of equally brave Irishmen who had also helped defend the castle. These were bound in pairs and thrown from the castle into the estuary. Today the outer fabric is complete enough to be wonderfully impressive, although war and nature have taken their toll of the internal work. Of the Great Hall, where Edward I celebrated his belated Christmas almost 700 years ago, only a single roof arch remains.

Within the town itself there is nothing of comparable age to the castle – except, of course, for the small part of the church that remains from the abbey and so pre-dates the castle. It is, however, a delightful place, with rows of tidy cottages, chiefly from the eighteenth and nineteenth centuries. The oldest house is Aberconwy House on the corner of Castle Street and High Sreet. This dates from the fifteenth century, at roughly the time when Henry VII was founding the Welsh line of kings, the Tudors. It is certainly not a humble cottage, more probably being typical of the style of the town's merchants. With its elaborate entrance and the

Telford's suspension bridge and the castle, Conwy

single overhang it has a distinctly Spanish look. The site is now in the hands of the National Trust and houses an exhibition on Conwy's history as well as a bookshop. Farther up Castle Street is the *Black Lion*, an elegant, gabled house which has been an inn since the eighteenth century, but was built in the late sixteenth century as the town house of the local vicar. Dating from the same period is Plas Mawr, which lies between High Street and the Terrace Cottages. This is a much grander building, reflecting the increased prosperity of both town and country, and is considered to be the finest Elizabethan town house in North Wales with much of the carved oak panelling and ceiling plaster being original. The house is owned by the Royal Cambrian Academy of Art and is open to the public in the summer months. From the upper part of the house there is a fine view of the town. From an architectural point of view, however, perhaps the best building in the town is close to the castle itself, Telford's road bridge. Before its construction the river, which had so effectively formed a barrier to invading armies, was proving an equally formidable barrier to travellers to and from Ireland. During the late eighteenth and early nineteenth centuries the town had prospered from the travellers, with a number of inns springing up to cater for their needs, and a ferry service across the river. The crossing was dangerous, due to the tidal races, and when in 1806, on Christmas Day, 13 of 15 passengers died in a capsize the town realised that unless something was done its prosperity would dwindle as the travellers moved south to cross at the bridges of Llanrwst and Betws-y-Coed. The latter had been constructed by a Scottish engineer, Thomas Telford, who was invited to design a road bridge at Conwy. He proposed a causeway linking the Deganwy bank to a small island in the estuary, and a suspension bridge from there to the castle rock, and work started in 1822. When completed the river crossing comprised a 2,015-foot embankment and a 327-foot span. The chain supports are pairs of stone turrets 42 feet high with the roadway passing through an arch between them. The design of the castellated towers was clearly in deference to the position of the bridge, close up to the castle walls, and Telford seems to have been entirely successful. Certainly his bridge is more in keeping with the medieval structure than either the railway bridge or the new road bridge that flank it. The railway bridge is the work of Robert Stephenson, and was completed in 1846, 20 years after the completion of Telford's bridge. Stephenson too showed respect for the setting, giving crenellations and arrow slits to the massive towers that held the bridge. The bridge itself is tubular, having been constructed in sections and floated down river before being hoisted into position. It is an interesting design, but ' lacks the elegance of Telford's bridge. Both the new road and rail bridges required entrances to the town proper, and the walls were breached – interestingly for the first time since construction – in several places. Telford pushed his roadway through a wall tower, to produce the Bangor arch, which does not appear in the least bit out of place, and Stephenson, not to be outdone, breached the wall raising the whole wall structure to form a beautiful pointed archway.

Our journey is over. There is not the satisfaction of completing a big-name route, such as the Pennine Way, but those who have completed the journey will have satisfaction of a different kind. They will have explored from end to end a country of legend and history with fine peaks and good walking.

Appendix I

The Land of Wales

Wales as a whole is a country of mainly Palaeozoic rocks, Palaeozoic being the name given to a geological era which began about 600 million years ago with the Cambrian period, the earliest period from which fossil remains are commonly preserved. The Cambrian period was succeeded by the Ordovician about 500 million years ago, the Silurian period, ending about 400 million years ago, finishing the Lower Palaeozoic. These rocks are the basis of central and north Wales, indeed it was here that they were first studied, the names Silurian and Ordovician deriving from tribes of ancient Britons who inhabited Wales.

The Lower Palaeozoic rocks are sediments laid down in a major sea basin, a geosyncline or downfold in the earth's crust, which, in general, subsides as sediment is deposited and precedes the uplift of fold mountains. The downfold had a NE–SW trend over central and northern Wales, with land to the north-west and south-east, and was formed in the subsiding pre-Cambrian base. Pre-Cambrian is the generic name given to rocks older than those of the Palaeozoic era. In the Ordovician there was volcanic activity in many parts of north Wales, for instance Cader Idris and Snowdon, much of the Ordovician rock in those areas being volcanic in origin.

The Lower Palaeozoic deposition was followed, and ended, by an increase in intensity of the 'Caledonian' earth movements that elevated the land mass of north, central and south-west Wales, the sea retreating and establishing the sedimentation basins in which the Old Red Sandstone of the Brecon Beacons and surrounding areas in south Wales was deposited. These deposits commenced with rocks of the Devonian period, beginning 400 million years ago. In north Wales the earth movements elevated the area into a huge mountain range, the structure being influenced by the old pre-Cambrian masses of Anglesey and the Bangor/Padarn ridges in the north-west, and the tough Cambrian rocks of the Harlech Dome, which acted, to an extent, as resistant barriers against which the softer sedimentary rocks were folded. As always erosion followed the uplift, the mountains of north Wales being worn down as the limestones of the Carboniferous period, that succeeded the Devonian, were being laid down below a clear, shallow sea at a time when the climate was warm and humid, the vegetation luxuriant.

Further earth movements followed, the mountains of south Wales being uplifted and folded, while rocks of the Permian, last of the Upper Palaeozoic periods, and Triassic and Jurassic, of the Mesozoic era, were deposited beneath seas in what are now Clwyd and southern Dyfed. Little is known of the geological history of Wales from this time until the Ice Age of the Pleistocene period which began only about two million years ago. It may have been under the sea during the Cretaceous period, as southern England was, though no deposits exist. Perhaps they were eroded away at a later time. However it was during this period – the Tertiary period – that the form we see today was established. The unknown Tertiary period processes produced a gently undulating, dissected plateau (the author suggests that the wayfarer repeats this continuously as he climbs Pen-yr-ole-wen!) with apparently little regard for different rock types or their structure. For instance, the river systems have little relationship to their underlying geological structure, and appear to have been superimposed. The courses have adapted as different geological structures have been encountered due to erosion and uplifts. Such 'pulsed' history shows itself in 'neck-points', waterfalls and terraces. The (lower) Clun-gwyn waterfall on the River Mellte is an example of this rejuvenation of erosion.

As the Tertiary period passed the climate deteriorated, arctic conditions eventually prevailing during the Great Ice Age. At that time most of Wales, indeed most of Britain, was covered by a sheet of ice that, at its maximum when even the hills were submerged, was several thousand feet in thickness. The last glaciers retreated only about 10,000 years ago, although truly arctic conditions had been intermittent towards the end of the age, with occasional periods of plant growth and animal habitation.

Glaciation began with local ice caps on the mountain summits, from which glaciers developed occupying the upland valleys,

descending to lower ground and merging with others to form
continuous ice sheets, known as piedmont ice, which spread over
the lowland plains. The existing landforms governed the movements
of the glaciers in general, and so the ice utilised the major valleys.
From the mountainous centre of Wales there was, broadly, a radial
dispersion with the ice flowing eastward to the Shropshire-Cheshire
plain, or the Hereford plain (Severn, Wye, Usk, Dee, Vyrnwy) and
westward to Cardigan Bay and St. George's Channel (Teifi, Aeron,
Ystwyth, Rheidol, Dyfi), as well as southward to the Bristol
Channel (Tawe, Neath, Taff, Ebbw) and northward to the Irish Sea.
Within this major area were minor centres where ice accumulated
and dispersed. Wales today is much as it was at the end of the Ice
Age, and signs of glacial erosion are evident along our route, being
a main part of the grandeur of the Welsh mountain scenery. The
sources of the glaciers were the amphitheatre-shaped hollows on the
mountain sides known generally as cirques or corries, but as cwms
in Wales. Cwm Cau on the side of Cader Idris is an excellent
example. Many of these hollows have lakes dammed by the moraine
of retreating glaciers. Llyn Cau in Cwm Cau is a good example.
Associated features are also widespread: aretes are sharp, rock
ridges, usually found where cirques erode back to back, a good
example being Bristly Ridge on Glyder Fach. There are also screes,
steep slopes of frost-shattered, loose rocks, well displayed around
Snowdon; valleys over-deepened by glacier action giving them a
characteristic U-shaped profile with near vertical walls and bevelled
spurs where the ends of ridges that ran into the valley have been
worn away, as for instance on the southern slopes of Glyder Fawr;
hanging valleys where tributaries entered the over-deepened valleys
with, now, a marked change in gradient, such as the Afon Dudodyn
joining the Llanberis Pass; ribbon lakes occupying rock basins,
hollows left by the irregular erosion of the valley floor.

As a result of glacial and melt-water erosion large amounts of
rock debris were removed and deposited over the valley floors and
coastal plains of Wales. The debris usually comprised stones of
varying shapes and sizes, randomly scattered in unstratified clay and
sand – boulder clay. More localised deposits, originating from the
edges or front of a glacier, are known as lateral and terminal

moraine respectively, and these often form a barrier across a valley mouth, or a corrie (cwm), marking the final position of the glacier. Lakes form behind such barriers, a good example being Llyn y fan fach formed behind a cirque barrier.

Apart from the glacial deposits our route starts in an area with the youngest strata found in Wales – the Trias and Lias of the early Jurassic period covering the Vale of Glamorgan. Northwards we pass into the eastern part of the South Wales Coalfield, and through towns that developed around the coal, clay and iron ore associated with the Carboniferous rocks of the escarpment – the carboniferous limestone, millstone grit and coal measures. The coal seams and millstone grit are found in cycles and are intermixed with sandstone indicating a subsidence and subsequent silting up. Because of the cyclical deposition the millstone grit was known as Farewell Rock, for when it was reached there was little workable coal left on the seam.

Welsh coal may be divided into three main types. The bituminous coals are relatively soft with a high amount of volatile matter making them good house, gas and coking coals. Anthracites are hard, stone coals with a low amount of volatile matter which burn smokelessly at high temperatures, and are unsuitable for coke. Steam coals are intermediate. The distribution of types is, roughly, governed by the tendency for lower seams at any place to be the most anthracitic, and for a particular seam to become more anthracitic towards the north and west. Thus we have the bituminous coals in the south and east, and the steam coals in the centre.

Another productive portion of the coal measures was the brick clay underlying the coal seam, which represents the muddy beds in which forests of the coal measure had their roots, the coal seam itself, of course, being formed of the compressed, decaying vegetation.

To the north of the Coalfield and the limestone outcrops there is a wide area of gently dipping Old Red Sandstone. Our route takes in the Black Mountains, Brecon Beacons and Mynydd Ddu, the heights of which are part of a steep northern escarpment which runs almost continuously for many miles. The main bulk of the escarpment is formed of resistant brownstones, capped by pebbly plateau beds. The resultant tops are as barren as any country encountered further north. However, in contrast to the north the relatively fertile red marls of the low-lying areas mean that agriculture is more varied than on the northern moors. The effects of glaciation abound, and are particularly fine in the series of sculpted valleys running north from the Beacons scarp.

Our route moves south of the escarpment of Fforest Fawr, to the 'waterfall' country, an area of millstone grit and carboniferous limestone on the northern edge of the coal measures. The limestone is soluble in rainwater, dilute carbonic acid, and permeable due to the jointed structure of the rock, with horizontal bedding planes and vertical joints. Thus the rock allows water to penetrate and dissolve its way out and in doing so to create the features typical of such areas. Where the water disappears underground the entrance often becomes an enlarged hole known as a 'sink hole' or 'swallet hole'. Commonly whole rivers can disappear underground, leaving a 'dry valley', which adds the erosional effects of the river to the action of the rainwater already underground. Both the Hepste and the Mellte have left dry beds, the latter disappearing at the famous Porth yr Ogof cave. Another typical feature of the soluble and permeable nature of the rock is cave formation, the most famous, but by no means the only, ones being those at Dan yr Ogof.

Rivalling the underground caves and dry valleys in the limestone are the waterfalls and rapids of the Hepste and Mellte. Both rivers have steep profiles, the falls being due to erosion rejuvenation, as mentioned previously, and to fault lines. At Sgwd yr Eira on the Hepste, the most famous fall, a band of shale, softer than the grit above and below it, has been eroded away so that it is possible to walk behind the fall. The fall originated downstream where a fault occurs, and has cut back to its present position. More complex fault movements have taken place at the sites of Sgwd Isaf Clun-gwyn and Sgwd Clun-gwyn on the Mellte.

North of the last sandstone scarp, of Mynydd Ddu, we reach an area rich in mineralisation, as indeed are most of the Welsh Palaeozoic rocks. Lead, zinc, copper and iron ores – commonly these are galena, zinc blende, copper pyrites and haematite

respectively – exist as veins, especially in the Silurian rocks of
mid-Wales and the Carboniferous rocks of north and south Wales.
Once lead was mined very profitably in Cardiganshire (now in
Dyfed), but it is now no longer economic. There are many disused
mines on our route, the best being at Cmwystwyth, evidence of
Wales' great mineral wealth. The current absence of mining activity
has returned the land to its former state. In general the area is a
moorland plateau with rounded hills dissected by river valleys. The
moors are often bleak with soils allowing only sheep farming, and
the country becomes more wild and rugged towards and about
Plynlimon. This wild sparsely populated upland with deep winding
valleys and numerous tributaries, together with abundant rainfall,
has led to the development of the area as reservoir country. The
main valleys associated with the reservoirs are those of the Elan and
the Claerwen, near Rhayader.

North of the Dyfi the igneous rocks that have occasionally been
seen as bare crags in mid-Wales are shown in their full glory on
Cader Idris. Igneous rocks are those that have cooled from molten
magma, often released during earth movements. Magma which
reaches the surface, usually as lava from volcanoes, and cools forms
rocks known as extrusive igneous rocks, while magma which cools
without reaching the surface, and so within the rock cover, forms
intrusive igneous rocks. Usually in an area where volcanic activity
has occurred both types are found.

The rocks of the Cader Idris region originated in the extensive,
shallow sea in which the Ordovician sediments were deposited.
Volcanic islands existed in this area which, when active, spread their
products over the normal sediments periodically. Earth movements,
and subsequent erosion, particularly during the Ice Age have
produced the escarpment we see today.

To the north of the Mawddach estuary is the Harlech Dome, an
anticlinal formation of Cambrian sediments bordered by the sea to
the west and a ring of Ordovician volcanic rocks inland. These
Cambrian rocks are the oldest that our route traverses, and are hard
grits that have produced a wild, mountainous country.

The best examples of the slate industry in Wales are the quarries
and mines around Blaenau Ffestiniog, on the north-eastern edge of

the Harlech Dome. Slate is one of the products of a third rock classification – metamorphic rocks. These are formed by the action of pressure or temperature on either sedimentary or igneous rocks, producing a rock completely different from the original. In the case of slate, soft shales and mudstones have, under pressure, had their constituent particles both flattened and re-orientated, and are said to adopt a 'slaty cleavage' allowing them to be split in one direction while remaining strong in all others. The process is independent of the age of the rock. In the case of the Blaenau slates the original rock was lower Ordovician strata. North of Blaenau there are impressive slate workings at Llanberis and Bethesda. Here, however, the eye is drawn, both geologically and scenically, to the mountains around Snowdon.

Northern Snowdonia as a whole is in the form of a NE–SW aligned syncline, a complex of minor folds within an overall downfold. There are pre-Cambrian and Cambrian rocks to the north-west, the Cambrian reappearing in the Harlech Dome to the south-east. The region between is of Ordovician rock, a composite structure with a complicated arrangement of folds and troughs without general trends. The folds are particularly well seen at Cwm Idwal, and below the summit of Snowdon itself.

The landscape we now see has been greatly influenced by glaciation, and excellent examples of its effects abound, one of the best being the valley of Nant Ffrancon between the Glyders and the Carneddau. This has the typical U-shaped cross-section with many cwms excavated into its sides. The passage of the ice, carrying rock debris, scarred the surface, and an outcrop scoured in this way is often left as an elongated, rounded boulder. Such formations occur often enough to have been named – roches moutonnées – and a fine example is to be found beneath Tryfan at the head of the Nant Ffrancon pass.

Our route finishes by traversing the Carneddau, the most pastoral, because it is the least igneous-dominated, of the Snowdonian ranges. Its rounded hills, Pen-yr-ole-wen notwithstanding, offer a gentle way of reaching Conwy and the sea.

This survey of the geology/geography of Wales is, of course,

immediately indicative of the economic history of the country. The
fertile coastal plain attracted early settlers, but it was the country's
mineral wealth that dominated its economy, with the exploitation of
metal ores, coal and slate. Interestingly the driving force for the
exploitation was rarely Welsh in origin. Indeed the social history of
the Welsh is one of exploitation by others, usually the English .
Since our route crosses the South Wales Coalfield, the mining
country of mid-Wales and the slate 'fields' of north Wales the
history of these industries is dealt with in the main body of the book.
With the decline of the mineral-based industries Wales has returned
to an agriculturally-based economy supplemented, in certain areas,
to a major extent by tourism and the craft industries that spring up
around it. Both industries are affected by climate, and the country's
weather is very easily summarised. Wales is wet. The upland areas,
those taken by the route described, collect a high proportion of the
annual rainfall. The Snowdon area receives an annual average of
around 160 inches of rain, most of the upland areas receiving
around 100 inches. To this high rainfall must be added the effect of
strong winds, prevailing south-west, and the fact that the proximity
of the upland masses to the sea means that the decrease in
temperature with altitude is more marked in Wales than is general,
at around 0.3°C (0.5°F) per 100 feet (30m).

The upland combination of cold, high winds and rainfall together
with generally inadequate drainage have produced a poor soil and a
land incapable of sustaining intense and varied plant growth. It is
likely that in pre-Roman times the land was deeply forested, but
only to 2,000 feet. Above that the moorland was thinly covered
with a limited plant life, now limited almost exclusively to grass by
sheep grazing, the only economic use in agricultural terms. In the
lowlands the rainfall is still high, but the drainage and soil are
better, allowing a greater variety of plant life and a more varied
agriculture. Those who habitually travel along the high land of
Wales may miss this more pleasing aspect of the country, and
believe that sparse grass and conifer are all that Wales has to offer.
To show that such is not the case our route has been directed south
of the Old Red Sandstone of Fforest Fawr to the limestone country
around Ystradfellte, where there is not only some very fine scenery,
but the typical flora of carboniferous limestone.

Appendix II

Accommodation

The route described in the book, being unofficial, is not supported by a network of hostels and camp sites such as has arisen around other long-distance footpaths. Indeed the failure to create an official Cambrian Way led to the demise of the Gerddi Bluog Youth Hostel on the western Rhinogs. Despite that the route is well supported by Youth Hostels, at least from the Brecon Beacons National Park northwards, although there are two sections, Ystumtuen to Kings and Kings to Ffestiniog, where detours are required if the walker is not to have long days. However, in each case there is a mid-point town – Machynlleth and Barmouth – where accommodation is obtainable.

Between Cardiff and the Brecon Beacons the situation is not as good. The loss of the hostel at Crickhowell means that there is now a long day between Capel-y-ffin and Llwyn-y-Celyn, and there are no hostels to the south of Capel-y-ffin. However between Cardiff and Abergavenny the route passes through many towns all of which offer bed and breakfast accommodation, at least.

For the backpacker the situation is less clear. In Snowdonia camp sites abound and some are in excellent positions – at (739121) below Cader Idris, and at (672604) below Tryfan, for example – but to the south they are less frequent and less well situated. Indiscriminate camping cannot be encouraged, and can be easily criticised on the grounds of environmental pollution, not to mention fire risk etc. In the early section of the walk where landowners are more accessible such camping should not, in any case, be necessary. On balance the backpacker should make his own effort to ensure continued access on to the hills by not antagonising landowners, conservationists etc. by stopping wherever he pleases. He should use his tent, with the landowners' permission, until the hostels start and then use these until North Wales is reached where he can safely return to camping.

Below is a list of hostels on, or close to, the route.

Capel-y-ffin (250328) in the Vale of Ewyas above Abergavenny.
About 1½ miles east of the route.

Llwyn-y-Celyn (973225) on the western flank of the Brecon
Beacons, north of the *Storey Arms*. On the route.

Ystradfellte (925127) about ¾ mile south of the village of
Ystradfellte. On the route.

Llanddeusant (776245) in the 'village' of Llanddeusant. On the
route.

Bryn Poeth Uchaf (796439) east and above the village of
Rhandirmwyn. About 1 mile east of the route.

Ty'n-y-Cornel (751534) in the upper Doethie valley. On the route.

Dolgoch (806561) in the Tywi valley north of Llyn Brianne. About
3 miles east of the route.

Blaencaron (713608) in the valley of Afon Groes on the western
edge of Elenydd. About 2 miles west of the route.

Ystumtuen (735786) 1 mile north of Devil's Bridge. On the route.

Corris (753080) in the village of Corris in the valley of the Afon
Dulas north of Machynlleth. About 3 awkward miles east of the
route.

Kings (683161) above the Mawddach river north of Cader Idris.
About 1½ miles north-east of the route.

Llanbedr (585267) in the village of Llanbedr on the A496 north of
Barmouth. About 3½ miles west of the route.

Harlech (580308) in the village of Harlech. About 5½ miles west of
the route.

Ffestiniog (704427) in the village of Llan Ffestiniog. On the route.

Bryn Gwynant (641513) on the edge of Llyn Gwynant. About 1
mile east of the route.

Pen-y-Pass (647556) at the head of the Llanberis Pass. On the
route.

Idwal Cottage (648603) at the head of Nant Ffrancon pass. On the
route.

Ro Wen (747721) on the eastern slopes of the Carneddau. About 1
mile south-east of the route.

The positions of the hostels given above, that is 'on' or 'off' route,
should not, of course, be taken literally. Since there is no marked

route the hostels cannot be on or off it. The description is meant only as a guide to the position of the hostel relative to the book-route.

The list is not exhaustive in Snowdonia, where slight variations of route by different walkers would allow the hostels of Snowdon Ranger, Llanberis, Betws-y-Coed, Lledr Valley and Capel Curig to be used.

Appendix III

Rights of Way and Access

Those long-distance footpaths in Britain that have been designated by Act of Parliament (that is the Countryside Commission's 'official' footpaths) have benefited from the creation, where necessary, of rights of way and the maintenance of paths so as to ensure that the walker may use them free of any hindrance. The route described in this book has not been designated as official and, in the foreseeable future, is unlikely to be so designated. It is important, therefore, that the walker should be aware of his rights on the route and, equally important, of his obligations also, both to the owner of the land that he crosses and to those who follow him. Though termed a 'right' of way, the walker should also see the pathway as a privilege granted to him by the landowner. He should treat the land with respect, bearing in mind that it is up to him how the next walker will be treated.

A large fraction (more than two-thirds) of the described route is over public rights of way. The right of passage depends upon the type of 'highway' described by the way. On a public footpath the right of passage is on foot. On a bridleway there are additional rights of passage on horseback or cycle. These two rights of way are marked in red on the Ordnance Survey 1:50,000 series maps (particularly the Landranger series which has definitive rights of way marked) and in green on the 1:25,000 series maps. Legal orders changing rights of way are usually notified to the O.S. but some do not get through, such as the diversions in connection with the Trawsfynydd power station and Llyn Stwlan.

In addition to these two types of highway there are also 'roads used as public paths' which may allow vehicle passage, and 'byways open to all traffic' which certainly do.

Public roads are shown in various colours on the O.S. maps according to status, but there are many public roads that are uncoloured. These 'white' roads are mostly untarred stony roads or green lanes, and are indistinguishable, on the maps, from private roads. It is, however, usually safe to infer that a white road is public if public paths are shown as terminating on it. The route follows several of these white roads, checks on their status having been made at county offices.

Rights of way have become established by prolonged usage with the acquiesence of the owner of the land, and must be on a defined route. Although many public paths exist over open country it is common for the way to be less defined. When the survey of rights of way was being conducted from which the definitive maps were derived, uncertainty as to the line of paths across open land often led to their being marked only to the edge of the open country. This was not thought to matter as the facility to roam at large was never disputed. Problems can arise, however, if right of access is disputed. In English law one cannot establish a right to roam at large by continued usage with acquiesence of the owner, as one can with defined rights of way. The difference between a 'right of way' and a 'right of access' is worth mentioning here. On the former the highway authority has a duty to maintain the highway and to keep it free from obstruction. No such duty applies over the area of land to which the public may have right of access, so that one cannot expect bridges everywhere over streams or the clearing of gorse and bracken. There are some categories of open country where the public has a legal right of access and this has considerable relevance to the described route.

1 *Urban Commons*
Under the Law of Property Act 1925 the public acquired a right of access for 'air and exercise' to commons that at the time were administered by borough or urban district councils. At the south-end of the route this includes Mynydd Machen and a long line of commons from Twmbarlwm near Risca to just south of the Blorenge above Abergavenny. At the northern end Conwy mountain and the traverse path leading to the Sychnant Pass are on commons in former urban districts.

2 *Crown Commons*
Under the same Act owners of common land were able to make a

deed of declaration which gave the public the same rights of access over commons in former rural districts. In 1932 this procedure was adopted by the Crown Commissioners for its extensive commons in the rural districts of Wales (though not for England). Sections of the route run over public-access crown commons, including the northern part of the Carneddau, Plynlimon, the northern Rhinogs, Moelwyn Mawr, the Teifi Pools and the land to the north of these, around Domen Milwyn.

3 'The Birmingham Clauses'
The route passes over the fringe of the gathering grounds of the Elan Valley reservoirs, which are covered by the famous 'Birmingham Clauses' giving the public 'a privilege at all times to enjoy air, exercise and recreation'.

4 National Trust Land
Several sections of the route traverse National Trust Land which is open to the public. The longest stretch of non-definitive route on National Trust Land is the high parts of the Carneddau from the Ogwen Valley to Drum, but sections also exist on Sugar Loaf and Pen y Fan in the Brecon Beacons National Park.

5 Rural Commons
Commons in areas administered by rural district councils before 1974 do not normally provide a legal right of access for the public, unless there is a Law of Property Act deed. In practice the facility to roam is virtually never disputed and it has long been the policy of the amenity organisations such as the Ramblers' Association and Commons, Open Spaces and Footpath Preservation Society to press for legislation to legalise the public's use of rural commons, as recommended by the Royal Commission on Commons in 1958.

The longest stretch of rural common on the route is the Black Mountains section from Bal Mawr via the Twmpa, Waun Fawr and Pen Allt-mawr to Table Mountain near Crickhowell. All this is very well known as a mountain walk. Other sections are Mynydd Llangynydr and the Black Mountain (Mynydd Ddu) Common. In the central part of the Beacons are two sections of Fforest Fawr

(Great Forest in the old meaning of the word). The common status provisionally registered is disputed by the Allotment Holders of the Great Forest who claim joint ownership, an unusual arrangement, whereas most commons are owned by a lord of the manor and many farmers have common grazing rights. Potential problems on this section led to the suggestion in the main text that the walker should seriously consider avoiding crossing Fforest Fawr in favour of a detour on definitive paths *via* the waterfall country.

For all the other mentioned commons there is *de facto* access and no one would dream of trying to contact the owner to ask permission to walk over them.

6 *Cardiff*
Cardiff City has no definitive map as yet but the route follows publicly maintained paths and roads or is through public parks or on a council-owned former canal towpath open to the public.

There remain a few sections of the route, all on high ground, that do not fall into any of the above categories but which are open country with *de facto* access, that is to say that so far as is known walkers are not denied access as long as they act in a reasonable manner. The sections are over land which comes within the definition of open country in part V of the National Parks and Access to the Countryside Act 1949. Amongst the type of country in the definition are mountain and moorland. The Act did not give the public any right of access to open country, but provided the means whereby local authorities could secure public access in cases where it was denied or agreed by the parties to be desirable. A public right of access can be obtained either by agreement or compulsorily by order. The Act provides for possible limitations on access such as for periods of grouse shooting, and enables the payment of compensation for allowing access and the provision of a warden service. Although several access agreements have been made in the Peak District, none has so far been made in Wales. It is to be hoped that walkers in Wales will not act in such a manner that access will be denied, precipitating the need to secure access with all the acrimony that would inevitably follow such an action.

Outside all these categories are a very limited number of route sections that follow waymarked routes negotiated by the National Park authorities, including 'courtesy paths' over private land (for instance, the route to the Glyders from Pen-y-Pass traverses land in the ownership of Mrs. Esme Kirby); unofficial diversions, where the obvious and distinct path does not follow the right of way, though it traverses the same land between the same two points; and paths whose status is uncertain because while they appear to be in general public use they are not on the definitive maps and should be claimed at any review.

Index